# Teach This Poem, Volume II

Instill a love of poetry in your classroom with the illuminating and inviting lessons from *Teach This Poem*. Copublished with the Academy of American Poets (AAP), the leading champion of poets and poetry in the United States, this book is an accessible entry point to teaching poetry and fostering a poetic sensibility in the classroom. Each lesson follows a consistent format, with a warm-up activity to introduce the chosen poem, pair shares, whole class synthesis, related resources, oral readings, and extension activities. Curated by the AAP, the poems are chosen with an eye toward fostering compassion and representing diverse experiences. Understanding that poetry is a powerful way of seeing the world, the volumes are organized thematically: Volume I is centered on the natural world and Volume II on equality and justice. Aligned with current standards and pedagogy, these lessons will inspire English teachers and their students alike.

Founded in 1934 in New York City, **The Academy of American Poets** is the nation's leading champion of American poets and poetry, with members in all fifty states. Its mission is to support American poets at all stages of their careers and to foster the appreciation of contemporary poetry.

**Madeleine Fuchs Holzer** was the Inaugural Educator in Residence at the Academy of American Poets, where she curated and created Teach This Poem. She has taught at high school and university levels, and has been an arts-in-education administrator. Her poetry and essays have appeared in several literary journals.

# Teach This Poem, Volume II
*Equality for All*

The Academy of American Poets and
Madeleine Fuchs Holzer

NEW YORK AND LONDON

Designed cover image: © Getty Images

First published 2026
by Routledge
605 Third Avenue, New York, NY 10158

and by Routledge
4 Park Square, Milton Park, Abingdon, Oxon, OX14 4RN

*Routledge is an imprint of the Taylor & Francis Group, an informa business*

© 2026 The Academy of American Poets and Madeleine Fuchs Holzer

The right of The Academy of American Poets and Madeleine Fuchs Holzer to be identified as authors of this work has been asserted in accordance with sections 77 and 78 of the Copyright, Designs and Patents Act 1988.

All rights reserved. No part of this book may be reprinted or reproduced or utilised in any form or by any electronic, mechanical, or other means, now known or hereafter invented, including photocopying and recording, or in any information storage or retrieval system, without permission in writing from the publishers.

*Trademark notice:* Product or corporate names may be trademarks or registered trademarks, and are used only for identification and explanation without intent to infringe.

ISBN: 978-1-032-52927-1 (hbk)
ISBN: 978-1-032-52269-2 (pbk)
ISBN: 978-1-003-40923-6 (ebk)

DOI: 10.4324/9781003409236

Typeset in Univers
by SPi Technologies India Pvt Ltd (Straive)

# Contents

| | |
|---|---|
| Foreword by Alberto Ríos | vii |
| Introduction by Madeleine Fuchs Holzer | x |
| **Chapter 1**  *One Nation Out of Many* | **1** |
| Introduction | 1 |
| "Ode to Sequoyah" by Alexander Posey | 3 |
| "Kumulipo" by Queen Lili'uokalani | 5 |
| "The Buttonhook" by Mary Jo Salter | 8 |
| "Amphibians" by Joseph O. Legaspi | 11 |
| "Lines Breaking" by José B. González | 13 |
| "América" by Richard Blanco | 16 |
| "Kissing in Vietnamese" by Ocean Vuong | 20 |
| "The Dream of Shoji" by Kimiko Hahn | 22 |
| "Red Brocade" by Naomi Shihab Nye | 24 |
| "Senior Discount" by Ali Liebegott | 27 |
| "Girls on the Town, 1946" by Rita Dove | 30 |
| "Haircut" by Elizabeth Alexander | 32 |
| "Crossing" by Jericho Brown | 35 |
| "Maps" by Yesenia Montilla | 38 |
| "Perhaps the World Ends Here" by Joy Harjo | 41 |
| "Survival Guide" by Joy Ladin | 44 |
| **Chapter 2**  *The Pursuit of Equality* | **47** |
| Introduction | 47 |
| "Lesson VIII: Map of North America" by Elizabeth Bradfield | 48 |
| "They Don't Love You Like I Love You" by Natalie Diaz | 51 |
| "Declaration" by Tracy K. Smith | 55 |
| "Dirt" by Kwame Dawes | 58 |
| "Making History" by Marilyn Nelson | 61 |
| "Won't You Celebrate With Me" by Lucille Clifton | 63 |
| "Black Laws" by Roger Reeves | 65 |
| "Imagine" by Kamilah Aisha Moon | 67 |
| "When Fannie Lou Hamer Said" by Mahogany L. Browne | 70 |
| "The Cabbage Butterfly" by Minnie Bruce Pratt | 74 |
| "Things We Carry on the Sea" by Wang Ping | 76 |

"Poem for the Poorest Country in the Western Hemisphere" by Danielle Legros Georges — 79
"A New National Anthem" by Ada Limón — 81
"Miss Mary Mack Introduces Her Wings" by Tyree Daye — 84
"I Want the Wide American Earth" by Carlos Bulosan — 86
"A House Called Tomorrow" by Alberto Ríos — 90

**Chapter 3**  *Afterword by Major Jackson* — 93

**Chapter 4**  *Glossary of Poetic Terms* — 96
  Types of Feet in Poetry — 103
  Types of Meters in Poetry — 104
  Four Examples of Quatrains in Poetry — 107
  Seven Examples of Repetition in Poetry — 108
  Types of Stanzas in Poetry — 110

Poet Biographies — 112

Credits — 119

Bibliography — 122

Acknowledgments — 126

Author Biography — 127

# Foreword by Alberto Ríos

Teaching poetry is an act of faith—a belief in the transformative power of words to shape minds, ignite imaginations, and foster a sense of shared humanity. When we invite poetry into the classroom, we open doors to new worlds, giving students the tools to articulate their thoughts and emotions in ways they never imagined possible. Poetry, with its unique ability to distill complex ideas into concentrated language, serves as both a mirror and a window, reflecting our individual experiences while offering glimpses into the lives and perspectives of others.

Written by a diverse array of voices, the poems in this book center around the themes of equality, justice, and unity. This polyphony captures the complexity of the American experience, reminding us that we are one nation out of many. These voices, each distinct yet harmonious, come together to form a rich tapestry speaking to the diversity and resilience of our nation. As students discover their love for poetry, they also discover their place within this larger narrative. They begin to see themselves as part of the ongoing story of America, a story that is still being written, by them, with every word they choose to put on the page.

In the classroom, poetry does more than just teach literary techniques; it teaches empathy, critical thinking, and the power of self-expression. When students engage with poetry, they learn to appreciate the nuances of language and the different ways in which a single idea can be expressed. They discover that there is no one right way to write a poem, just as there is no one right way to be human. This realization can be both liberating and empowering, particularly in a world that often seeks to impose rigid definitions of identity and success.

With that in mind, whatever problems you're going to face going forward, don't give up. Not giving up has always been my biggest advantage. I hope it will be yours as well.

These words of encouragement are particularly relevant for anyone who has ever struggled with writing, with understanding poetry, or with finding their own voice. Poetry is not always easy, and it can be frustrating to try to capture the perfect image or phrase. But the act of trying—of refusing to give up—is what makes us stronger, both as writers and as individuals. The perseverance required to craft a poem is the same perseverance that will carry students through the challenges they will face in life. Poetry teaches us that our words have power, and with that power comes the responsibility to use them wisely.

But we're all different, and I take that as a good thing. Everything is different, really—the whole world, with everything that's going on right now. The challenges we face are unprecedented. But in that strangeness, I still think there's a little bit of magic out there. It's shy, though, and you have to look for it. With so much loudness in the world, there seems to be no room for it.

Poetry is that magic. It's the quiet voice in the midst of chaos, the still point in a turning world. It's the pencil in the hand of a writer, which, like a magic wand, can create whole worlds out of nothing. I often ask people who the most powerful character is in *The Lord of the Rings*. Whatever the response, the real answer turns out to be simple and absolute. The most powerful person in *The Lord of the Rings* universe is J. R. R. Tolkien, the author of the books. We might have been tempted to say Gandalf or Galadriel or Elrond—or even Frodo. But, in stepping back, we realize that the author can make those characters do anything he wants them to do. He's writing the books. The author turns out to be everything.

The author could be you.

Here's something very useful to know: A regular #2 yellow pencil holds enough lead to write about 45,000 words, the size of a small novel. The entire *Lord of the Rings* series (including *The Hobbit*) has 576,459 words. Somebody actually counted them. The total number of words in the novels divided by the potential words in a simple pencil turns out to be 12.81. Essentially, that means the entire *Lord of the Rings* saga could be written with thirteen pencils. Thirteen. In this way, a pencil is incredibly powerful.

When students realize that they, too, hold the power of the author—the power to shape their own narratives—they begin to see the world differently. They understand that they are not just passive recipients of knowledge but active participants in the creation of meaning. Every pencil is filled with a book, and every student has the potential to be an author. Whether they are writing about their own experiences or imagining new worlds, they are contributing to the ongoing story of humanity.

As educators, our role is to nurture this potential, to encourage students to explore the possibilities of language and to take risks with their writing. We must remind them that their voices matter, that their stories are worth telling, and that they have the power to change the world—one word at a time. This book, with its focus on equality and justice, is a testament to the importance of these themes in both poetry and life. It challenges students to think critically about the world around them and to use their words to advocate for change.

Poetry, like language itself, is a personal property that can be acquired without much capital. When written, poetry is intellectual property that can be passed down, just like tangible assets. It is real. Just as there is no one way to see something, there is no one way to write a poem. The humanities—poetry included—give us the tools to see the world from multiple perspectives and to express our own unique and valuable viewpoints.

Poetry, and indeed art in general, should move us from where we're standing to what we're feeling. The humanities help us to be our best selves, to see the world more clearly, and to communicate effectively. They are the manner by which we are humans together, and they offer us choices—choices that are essential in a world that is constantly changing.

As we embark on this journey through the pages of this book, let us remember the power of words to shape our world. Let us encourage our students to write, to read, and to explore the vast possibilities of language. Let us remind them that they are the authors of their own stories and that with every word they write, they are helping to create a better future for us all.

In the words of Pablo Neruda, translated by Steve Kowit, "Only the poets are capable of putting [tyranny] against the wall and riddling [it] with the most deadly tercets." The task of poetry is not just to reflect the world but to transform it. Let us take up this task with courage and conviction, knowing that our words have the power to make a difference.

The world simply will not be the same as it was. What will be changed is up to us.

To the students, teachers, and readers of this book: You are it. You are who we're counting on, every one of you.

# Introduction by Madeleine Fuchs Holzer

*Teach This Poem, Volume 2: Equality for All* and its predecessor, *Teach This Poem, Volume 1: The Natural World* (Routledge, 2024), are based on a philosophy of perception developed by philosopher, psychologist, and educator John Dewey, author of *Art as Experience* (Perlgee, 1934).

According to Dewey:

> [T]o perceive, a beholder must create his own experience. And his creation must include relations comparable to those which the original producer underwent... The artist selected, simplified, clarified, abridged and condensed according to his interest. The beholder must go through these operations according to his point of view and interest.
>
> (Dewey, 1980, p. 54)

Maxine Greene built on Dewey's idea of perception in her lectures at Lincoln Center Institute when she coined the phrase "Aesthetic Education." She defined this as:

> an intentional undertaking designed to nurture appreciative, reflective, cultural, participatory engagements with the arts by enabling learners to notice what there is to be noticed, and to lend works of art their lives in such a way that they can achieve them as variously meaningful. When this happens, new connections are made in experience; new patterns are formed, new vistas are opened.
>
> (Greene, 2018, p. 6)

Although neither Dewey nor Greene addressed the study of poetry as an art form directly in these quotes, we have adapted their thoughts, while adding Jane Hirshfield's idea that poetic perception's work "is not simply the recording of inner or outer perception; it makes by words and music new possibilities of perceiving" (Hirshfield, 2015, p. 3).

We propose that when someone deeply engages with poetry, they experience, through mind and sense connections, its meaning and emotional impact, and understand the experience *beyond the words*. When this happens, not only can they apply what they have learned to poetry, but to learning in other disciplines—their poetic perception becomes a poetic sensibility.

The characteristics of poetic sensibility include:

- Keen sensitivity to the surrounding world (multisensory perception)
- Asking questions
- Identifying patterns
- Making both intuitive and logical connections
- A facility and passion for finding the right word or phrase to express feelings and meaning
- The use of imagination to connect these in unexpected ways.

Developing a poetic sensibility can help participants pursue discipline-based inquiries more fully and deeply, and open them to think creatively with more substance than they would otherwise. For poets, this sensibility is most likely intuitive; for readers, the experience of engaging deeply with poetry requires consciously understanding and using some of the same skills that poets use when they write.

We know participants bring different skill sets and styles to the classroom. All *Teach This Poem* lessons create an environment in which participants can experience poems through several entry points that begin with shared experiences. As a pedagogy that attempts to foster poetic sensibility while recognizing the importance of different perspectives, communities, and ways of learning, each lesson in *Teach This Poem* follows the same general trajectory:

- A warm-up related to the chosen poem that helps focus participants for the rest of the lesson.
- Careful noticing of a related resource from another genre or academic discipline. This gives participants an alternate entry point to the poem, as well as practice with noticing visual details.
- Using skills practiced with the related resource, an individual silent reading of the poem while creating a record of words, phrases, and poetic structures that stand out. This helps participants begin to think about what might be important in the poem, and provides a list of ideas they may be able to use as evidence in later discussions and writing.
- Oral readings of the poem, either by the poet in a video or two different participants. Listening participants add what they hear in the poem to what they saw on the page. This provides more ideas for evidence.
- Pair shares or small group discussions that give everyone a chance to speak and help participants who are uncomfortable speaking in a large group generate ideas. This adds more voices to large group discussions.

- A large group synthesis based on what participants have noticed in the poem and the related resource, guided by questions to open up multiple interpretations, as well as a shared synthesis.
- Optional extension activities.

While *Teach This Poem* can be adapted for use with younger or older participants, it is tailored for use with upper middle school and lower high school students. Each lesson includes questions about the featured poem, activities based on the aforementioned framework, and contextual information for the instructor.

It is our intention that educators tailor the lessons we provide to their participants' grade levels and needs. Above all, we encourage educators to use their own creativity as they adapt *Teach This Poem*, as only they can, for the specific participants they teach.

# 1 One Nation Out of Many

## Introduction

Engaging a group in meaningful conversations about race, equality, and justice can be both challenging and rewarding. As an educator, you have a unique opportunity to guide participants through these complex topics, helping them understand their place in a larger global context.

The National Council of Teachers of English (NCTE) states the following in their "Position Statement on Supporting Teachers and Students in Discussing Complex Topics":

> As educators, we not only have a responsibility toward our students to engage in societal dialogue; we also create space for students to develop their own sense of self, perspectives, opinions, and beliefs. It is critical that students develop the ability to effectively exercise critical thinking and respectful and productive discourse when exploring and discussing complex topics.

To get started, it's important to create an environment where participants feel safe and encouraged to express their thoughts. Setting clear ground rules for respectful dialogue is essential. This might include looking over the lessons and material prior to gathering, and flagging where more context around historical events, language choices, and societal issues would be appropriate for your group. Establishing an environment in which every voice matters and listening to different viewpoints should be a priority. By doing so, you're not just managing a classroom—you're building a community of mutual respect and curiosity.

This chapter will supply you with poetic histories and cultural perspectives that stem from direct experience. Understanding the individual experience present in each poem can help validate the diversity of voices that make up one global community. While lineage might mean something different to each person teaching and learning about poetry, the poems and poets featured in this chapter can provide a road map to your own version of a literary canon.

Use these lessons to help your group see the relevance of these topics beyond their own experiences and to foster a sense of shared humanity. By incorporating these resources and strategies into your teaching, you're setting the stage for educational and empowering discussions that will encourage participants to continue to grow into informed and empathetic individuals.

## "Ode to Sequoyah"
*by Alexander Posey*

The names of Waitie and Boudinot—
  The valiant warrior and gifted sage—
And other Cherokees, may be forgot,
  But thy name shall descend to every age;
The mysteries enshrouding Cadmus' name
Cannot obscure thy claim to fame.

The people's language cannot perish—nay,
  When from the face of this great continent
Inevitable doom hath swept away
  The last memorial—the last fragment
Of tribes,—some scholar learned shall pore
Upon thy letters, seeking ancient lore.

Some bard shall lift a voice in praise of thee,
  In moving numbers tell the world how men
Scoffed thee, hissed thee, charged with lunacy!
  And who could not give 'nough honor when
At length, in spite of jeers, of want and need,
Thy genius shaped a dream into a deed.

By cloud-capped summits in the boundless west,
  Or mighty river rolling to the sea,
Where'er thy footsteps led thee on that quest,
  Unknown, rest thee, illustrious Cherokee!

## Related Resource

## Activities

1. **Warm-up:** Who are some people that you admire in your community? Why? Make a list and share with a partner.
2. **Before Reading the Poem:** Look carefully at the lithograph of Sequoyah. What do you notice first? Focus on a detail in the lithograph and describe what you see to a partner.
3. **Reading the Poem:** Silently read "Ode to Sequoyah" by Alexander Posey. What do you notice about the poem? Note any words, phrases, or poetic structures that stand out to you and any questions you might have.
4. **Listening to the Poem:** Enlist two volunteers and listen as the poem is read aloud twice. What did you hear that you did not previously notice when you were reading the poem? Write down any additional words and phrases that stood out to you.
5. **Small Group Discussion:** Share what you noticed in the poem with your partner and another pair. Based on the details you just shared with your small group, how does the poem's speaker seem to feel about Sequoyah? What makes you think this?

Sequoyah.

John T. Bowen, *Se-Quo-Yah*, circa 1838. Lithograph, *History of the Indian Tribes of North America* by Thomas L. McKenney.

6. **Large Group Discussion**: What do you think is meant by the phrase "The people's language cannot perish"? Why do you think that Posey wanted to write an ode to Sequoyah?
7. **Extension for Grades 7–8**: Read this article about the Cherokee language. Create a presentation about what you learned.

8. **Extension for Grades 9–12**: Read or watch Joy Harjo's lecture "Mapping Indigenous Poetry." Create a presentation about what you learned or memorize and recite one of the poems mentioned in the lecture.

## More Context

### Article

Read more about Sequoyah and his accomplishments in Kristi Finefield's article for the Library of Congress, "Sequoyah: A Man of Letters." Finefield writes, "The man and the document turn out to be very impressive, indeed."

## Glossary Term

**Ode** a lyric address to an event, a person, or a thing that is not present.

## "Kumulipo"
### by Queen Liliʻuokalani

*Hawaiʻian creation chant*

At the time that turned the heat of the earth,
At the time when the heavens turned and changed,
At the time when the light of the sun was subdued
To cause light to break forth,
At the time of the night of Makalii (winter)
Then began the slime which established the earth,
The source of deepest darkness.
Of the depth of darkness, of the depth of darkness,
Of the darkness of the sun, in the depth of night,
>> It is night,
>> So was night born

O ke au i kahuli wela ka honua
O ke au i kahuli lole ka lani
O ke au i kukaiaka ka la.
E hoomalamalama i ka malama
O ke au o Makaliʻi ka po
O ka walewale hookumu honua ia
O ke kumu o ka lipo, i lipo ai
O ke kumu o ka Po, i po ai
O ka lipolipo, o ka lipolipo
O ka lipo o ka la, o ka lipo o ka po
>> Po wale hoi
>> Hanau ka po

## Related Resource

Video from the *Kumulipo*.

Lehua TV, "Kumulipo," 2019. Screenshot, YouTube.

## Activities

1. **Warm-up**: How do you think the world began? Free-write or draw for a few minutes. Share your writing or drawing with a partner.
2. **Before Reading the Poem**: Watch this animated video of an interpretation of the first twenty-eight lines of the *Kumulipo*. What do you notice? Where might this video have been taken? What makes you say that? How do you think this volcano formed?
3. **Reading the Poem**: Silently read "Kumulipo" by Queen Liliʻuokalani. What do you notice about the poem? Note any words, phrases, or poetic structures that stand out to you and any questions you might have.
4. **Listening to the Poem**: Enlist two volunteers and listen as the poem is read aloud twice. What did you hear that you did not previously notice when you were reading the poem? Write down any additional words and phrases that stand out to you.
5. **Small Group Discussion**: Share what you noticed in the poem with a small group of students. Based on the details you just shared with your small group, how does this poem begin? How does the poem's opening compare and contrast to the drawing or writing you did at the beginning of this lesson?
6. **Large Group Discussion**: In the poem, how does life develop? What is the relationship between light and darkness? Why might this poem/creation chant be considered sacred to Hawai'ians? Why do you think it was important that this poem was sung out loud? What other kinds of texts are typically chanted?
7. **Extension for Grades 7–8**: With a partner, reread the poem and then imagine and write the next ten lines, or write a poem in response to the question from the warm-up activity: How do you think the world began? With your partner, create an animation for your poem or an image from your poem. If you'd like, you can draw inspiration from the animated video you watched earlier. Share your animation or image with your peers.

8. **Extension for Grades 9–12**: Read "How Hawaiians Saved Their Language." In a small group, discuss: What is the importance of language? Why should language be protected? How might language impact you or your peers?

## More Context

### Book

The *Kumulipo* ("Beginning-in-deep-darkness") is the sacred creation chant of a family of Hawai'ian alii, or ruling chiefs. Composed and transmitted entirely in the oral tradition, its two thousand lines provide an extended genealogy proving the family's divine origin and tracing the family history from the beginning of the world.

Read more from the book *The Kumulipo: A Hawai'ian Creation Chant*, including a foreword and introduction about its history.

### Glossary Term

**Occasional poem** a poem written to document or provide commentary on an event.

## "The Buttonhook"
*by Mary Jo Salter*

President Roosevelt, touring Ellis Island
in 1906, watched the people from steerage
line up for their six-second physical.

Might not, he wondered aloud, the ungloved handling
of aliens who were ill infect the healthy?
Yet for years more it was done. I imagine

my grandmother, a girl in that Great Hall's
polyglot, reverberating vault
more terrible than church, dazed by the stars

and stripes in the vast banner up in front
where the blessed ones had passed through. Then she did too,
to a room like a little chapel, where her mother

might take Communion. A man in a blue cap
and a blue uniform—a doctor? a policeman?
(Papa would have known, but he had sailed

all alone before them and was waiting
now in New York; yet wasn't this New York?)—
a man in a blue cap reached for her mother.

Without a word (didn't he speak Italian?)
he stuck one finger into her mother's eye,
then turned its lid up with a buttonhook,

the long, curved thing for doing up your boots
when buttons were too many or too small.
You couldn't be American if you were blind

or going to be blind. That much she understood.
She'd go to school, she'd learn to read and write
and teach her parents. The eye man reached to touch

her own face next; she figured she was ready.
She felt big, like that woman in the sea
holding up not a buttonhook but a torch.

# One Nation Out of Many

## Related Resource

Line Inspection at Ellis Island.

Department of the Treasury, *Ellis Island, NY, Line Inspection of Arriving Aliens*, 1923. Photograph, National Archives.

## Activities

1. **Warm-up**: Look closely at the photograph of the inspection of immigrants at Ellis Island. Write down a detailed description of what you see and any questions you have about the photograph. How does it compare to times you have stood in line?
2. **Before Reading the Poem**: With a partner, discuss what you noticed. Explain how the photo seems similar to or different from your own experiences. Share your questions about the photo with the whole group.
3. **Reading the Poem**: Silently read "The Buttonhook" by Mary Jo Salter. What do you notice about the poem? Note any words, phrases, or poetic structures that stand out to you and any questions you might have.
4. **Listening to the Poem**: Watch Mary Jo Salter read her poem twice. What did you hear that you did not previously notice when you were reading the poem? Write down any additional words and phrases that stand out to you.
5. **Small Group Discussion**: This might be a good time to review the term "symbol." Take turns sharing what you noticed in the poem with a small group. What is similar and different about your observations? What in the poem connects to the image you looked at during the warm-up? What symbols do you notice in the poem? Based on these details, what can you tell about the people in the poem?

6. **Large Group Discussion**: What emotions can you identify in the poem? What emotions did you feel while reading the poem? How do you think the poet elicited these feelings? What techniques did she use? How are the video and text versions similar or different? Make sure to use evidence to support your answers.
7. **Extension for Grades 7–8**: Salter makes her grandmother a heroic figure by comparing her to the Statue of Liberty. Who would you compare to the Statue of Liberty? What object would they hold in the air? Write a poem about how the heroic figure you chose would lift the object you chose.
8. **Extension for Grades 9–12**: Read Emma Lazarus's poem, "The New Colossus," which was added to the Statue of Liberty in 1903, three years before the events imagined in Salter's poem. How does Salter reinterpret the symbol of the Statue of Liberty in "The Buttonhook"? Write an essay comparing the two interpretations or write a poem of your own about the Statue of Liberty.

## More Context

### Article

The National Park Service notes,

> Emma Lazarus was the poet who wrote "The New Colossus." Aside from writing, Lazarus was also involved in charitable work for refugees. At Ward's Island, she worked as an aide for Jewish immigrants who had been detained by Castle Garden immigration officials. She was deeply moved by the plight of the Russian Jews she met there and these experiences influenced her writing.

Read more about Emma Lazarus and the history of the Statue of Liberty and "The New Colossus."

## Glossary Term

**Symbol** an object or action that stands for something beyond itself.

## "Amphibians"
*by Joseph O. Legaspi*

In Greek, *amphibian* means
"on both sides of life."

As in: amphibians live
on land and in water.

As in: immigrants leave
lands and cross waters.

While amphibians lay
shell-less eggs,

immigrants give birth
to Americans.

In water, gilled tadpoles
sprout limbs. On land

amphibians develop lungs.
Immigrants develop lungs.

Breathe in pine, fuel
and cold atmosphere.

Amphibians' damp
skin oxygenates.

Immigrants toil
and slumber deathly.

Their colors brighten.
They camouflage.

They've been known to fall
out of the sky.

Completely at home
in the rain.

## Related Resource

Article on amphibians.

BITESIZE: BBC, "What Are Amphibians?" 2024. Screenshot, BBC.

## Activities

1. **Warm-up**: In a small group, consider the following questions: What does the word "migration" mean? In addition to people, do other living things in nature migrate? Why? Did your family or your ancestors migrate from one place to another? Why? Can you think of any migrations happening now? Why do you think they are happening?

2. 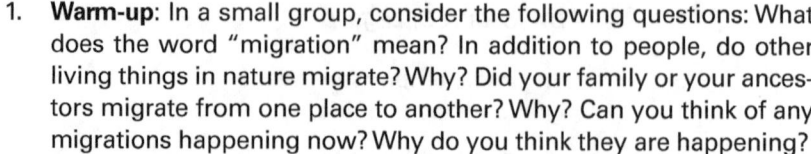 **Before Reading the Poem**: Read the BBC article, "What Are Amphibians?" to learn about amphibians and their context in the world. Keep a record of important words and phrases, as well as any words you do not understand. With a partner, discuss what you've learned about amphibians and any questions you might have. Try to figure out the meaning of new words together.

3. **Reading the Poem**: Silently read "Amphibians" by Joseph O. Legaspi. What do you notice about the poem? Note any words, phrases, or poetic structures that stand out to you and any questions you might have.

4. **Listening to the Poem**: Enlist two volunteers and listen as the poem is read aloud twice. What did you hear that you did not previously notice when you were reading the poem? Write down any additional words and phrases that stand out to you.

5. **Small Group Discussion**: What experiences might amphibians and immigrants have in common? Toward the end of the poem, Legaspi writes that "they" do something—do you think he means amphibians or immigrants? Why?

6. **Large Group Discussion**: Is Joseph O. Legaspi making a point about amphibians, immigrants, or both? Are amphibians a successful metaphor for immigrants? Cite evidence from your notes and discussions.

7. **Extension for Grades 7–8**: Do you agree with Legaspi that immigrants are like amphibians? Write a poem or paragraph explaining why.

8. **Extension for Grades 9–12**: Examine Legaspi's word choice in "Amphibians." In small groups, discuss: Does the poem speaker celebrate the idea of immigrants-as-amphibians, find it threatening, or both? Or something else? Write an essay explaining your conclusion using details from the poem as evidence.

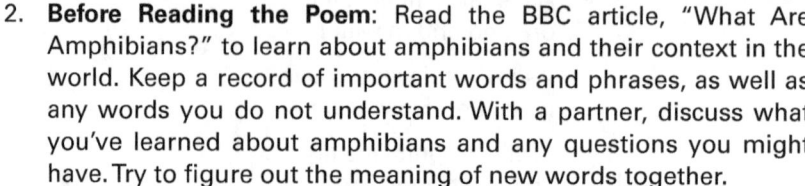

## More Context

### Poems

Read more poems exploring themes of immigration and heritage.

### Glossary Term

**Metaphor** a comparison between essentially unlike things or the application of a name or description to something to which it is not literally applicable.

## "Lines Breaking"
*by José B. González*

red pen in hand,
he tells me lines should
                            break
in order to empha-
                    size
certain words
like the ones in my family's history:
first-
    shift
second-
    shift
third-
    shift,

that words are like the earth
        shifting
back and
        forth during an
earth-
        quake
& that verse has more meaning
when words can teeter-
                    totter.
but as much as I try to
break the lines in their proper
                          poetic
                            places
there are words
that I cannot separate,
like father, mother and child,

words that I cannot break again
like father and leaving, mother and deserting,
child and hurting,

words that stay together all by themselves,
like immigration, isolation, desolation.

## Related Resource

### From *A Tale of Two Cities* by Charles Dickens

It was the best of times, it was the worst of times, it was the age of wisdom, it was the age of foolishness, it was the epoch of belief, it was the epoch of incredulity, it was the season of Light, it was the season of Darkness, it was the spring of hope, it was the winter of despair, we had everything before us, we had nothing before us, we were all going direct to Heaven, we were all going direct the other way,—in short, the period was so far like the present period, that some of its noisiest authorities insisted on its being received, for good or for evil, in the superlative degree of comparison only.

Excerpt from *A Tale of Two Cities*.

H. K. Browne, *A Tale of Two Cities* title page, 1859. Illustration, Wikimedia Commons.

### Activities

1. **Warm-up:** Silently read the first paragraph of *A Tale of Two Cities* by Charles Dickens.
2. **Before Reading the Poem:** What would happen if you tried to turn this paragraph into a poem without changing any words?

Experiment and see what happens. How would you break up the lines? What words would you not want to separate? Why?
3. **Reading the Poem**: Silently read "Lines Breaking" by José B. González. What do you notice about the poem? Note any words, phrases, or poetic structures that stand out to you and any questions you might have.
4. **Listening to the Poem**: Enlist two volunteers and listen as the poem is read aloud twice. What did you hear that you did not previously notice when you were reading the poem? Write down any additional words and phrases that stand out to you.
5. **Small Group Discussion**: What did you notice about the line breaks in the poem? How did they influence the way you read and heard the poem?
6. **Large Group Discussion**: How are the last four stanzas different from the rest of the poem? What happened to the line breaks? Why do you think this is the case? Is the poet making a connection between line breaks and immigration? Cite evidence from the poem to explain your thinking.
7. **Extension for Grades 7–8**: In small groups, share your *A Tale of Two Cities* poems from activity two. What happens when you change the placement of the words? Do you read them differently on the page? Do they sound different when read aloud? Is the meaning of the words the same, or does it change in some way?
8. **Extension for Grades 9–12**: Write a poem about a current event that you feel strongly about. Use what you have learned about line breaks to create stops, emphasis, and movement in your poem.

## More Context

### Essay

In her essay "Where It Breaks: Drama, Silence, Speed, and Accrual," the poet Dana Levin writes, "I want the line-break to tell me something about how a poem feels: where a speaker butts up against silence." She explains, "When my students read poems aloud, I insist they 'read' the line-breaks (this is not very popular). Feeling speaks where the line is silenced." Read the essay.

### Glossary Term

**Enjambment** the continuation of a sentence or clause across a poetic line break.

## "América"
*by Richard Blanco*

**I**

Although Tía Miriam boasted she discovered
at least half-a-dozen uses for peanut butter—
topping for guava shells in syrup,
butter substitute for Cuban toast,
hair conditioner and relaxer—
Mamá never knew what to make
of the monthly five-pound jars
handed out by the immigration department
until my friend, Jeff, mentioned jelly.

**II**

There was always pork though,
for every birthday and wedding,
whole ones on Christmas and New Year's Eves,
even on Thanksgiving Day—pork,
fried, broiled or crispy skin roasted—
as well as cauldrons of black beans,
fried plantain chips and *yuca con mojito*.

These items required a special visit
to Antonio's Mercado on the corner of 8th street
where men in *guayaberas* stood in senate
blaming Kennedy for everything—"*Ese hijo de puta*!"
the bile of Cuban coffee and cigar residue
filling the creases of their wrinkled lips;
clinging to one another's lies of lost wealth,
ashamed and empty as hollow trees.

**III**

By seven I had grown suspicious—we were still here.
Overheard conversations about returning
had grown wistful and less frequent.
I spoke English; my parents didn't.
We didn't live in a two story house
with a maid or a wood panel station wagon
nor vacation camping in Colorado.
None of the girls had hair of gold;
none of my brothers or cousins
were named Greg, Peter, or Marcia;
we were not the Brady Bunch.

None of the black and white characters
on Donna Reed or on Dick Van Dyke Show
were named Guadalupe, Lázaro, or Mercedes.
Patty Duke's family wasn't like us either—
they didn't have pork on Thanksgiving,
they ate turkey with cranberry sauce;
they didn't have *yuca*, they had yams
like the dittos of Pilgrims I colored in class.

## IV

A week before Thanksgiving
I explained to my *abuelita*
about the Indians and the Mayflower,
how Lincoln set the slaves free;
I explained to my parents about
the purple mountain's majesty,
"one if by land, two if by sea"
the cherry tree, the tea party,
the amber waves of grain,
the "masses yearning to be free"
liberty and justice for all, until
finally they agreed:
this Thanksgiving we would have turkey,
as well as pork.

## V

*Abuelita* prepared the poor fowl
as if committing an act of treason,
faking her enthusiasm for my sake.
*Mamà* set a frozen pumpkin pie in the oven
and prepared candied yams following instructions
I translated from the marshmallow bag.
The table was arrayed with gladiolus,
the plattered turkey loomed at the center
on plastic silver from Woolworths.
Everyone sat in green velvet chairs
we had upholstered with clear vinyl,
except Tío Carlos and Toti, seated
in the folding chairs from the Salvation Army.
I uttered a bilingual blessing
and the turkey was passed around
like a game of Russian Roulette.
"DRY," Tío Berto complained, and proceeded
to drown the lean slices with pork fat drippings
and cranberry jelly—"*esa mierda roja*," he called it.

Faces fell when *Mamá* presented her ochre pie—
pumpkin was a home remedy for ulcers, not a dessert.
Tía María made three rounds of Cuban coffee
then *Abuelo* and Pepe cleared the living room furniture,
put on a Celia Cruz LP and the entire family
began to *merengue* over the linoleum of our apartment,
sweating rum and coffee until they remembered—
it was 1970 and 46 degrees—
in *América*.
After repositioning the furniture,
an appropriate darkness filled the room.
Tío Berto was the last to leave.

## Related Resource

Thanksgiving illustration.

Louis John Rhead, *Harper's Bazar–Thanksgiving 1894*, 1894. Copy Slide, Library of Congress.

## Activities

1. **Warm-up**: Look carefully at the *Harper's Bazar* Thanksgiving cover, published in 1894. Write down what you notice about the cover, such as the colors, lines, and shapes. What does this image make you think of?
2. **Before Reading the Poem**: With a small group, share how you celebrate Thanksgiving or another holiday. Choose someone from your group to tell everyone the ways in which the group members celebrate.
3. **Reading the Poem**: Silently read "América" by Richard Blanco. What do you notice about the poem? Note any words, phrases, or poetic structures that stand out to you and any questions you might have.
4. **Listening to the Poem**: Enlist two volunteers and listen as the poem is read aloud twice. What did you hear that you did not previously notice when you were reading the poem? Write down any additional words and phrases that stand out to you.
5. **Small Group Discussion**: Take turns sharing what you noticed in the poem with a small group. What is similar or different about your observations? What can you learn about the speaker in the poem? Does this poem connect to the ways you celebrate Thanksgiving or another holiday? Why or why not?
6. **Large Group Discussion**: How is this poem similar to or different from the *Harper's Bazar* cover? What does the speaker of the poem seem to be saying about what it's like to move countries? Why might it be important to read about the experiences described in the poem?
7. **Extension for Grades 7–8**: Write and draw an illustrated essay about a family member or friend's celebration that you attended and remember vividly. Interview someone who was also there about the celebration. Add to or revise your essay to include the additional point of view.
8. **Extension for Grades 9–12**: What is the essence of Thanksgiving or another holiday? What should all celebrations contain? Write a persuasive essay on this subject.

## More Context

### Poems

Explore more poems by Indigenous poets such as Richard Calmit Adams, Joy Harjo, Lois Red Elk, M. L. Smoker, and more.

## Glossary Term

**Free verse**  poetry that isn't dictated by an established form or meter, often influenced by the rhythms of speech.

## "Kissing in Vietnamese"
*by Ocean Vuong*

My grandmother kisses
as if bombs are bursting in the backyard,
where mint and jasmine lace their perfumes
through the kitchen window,
as if somewhere, a body is falling apart
and flames are making their way back
through the intricacies of a young boy's thigh,
as if to walk out the door, your torso
would dance from exit wounds.
When my grandmother kisses, there would be
no flashy smooching, no western music
of pursed lips, she kisses as if to breathe
you inside her, nose pressed to cheek
so that your scent is relearned
and your sweat pearls into drops of gold
inside her lungs, as if while she holds you
death also, is clutching your wrist.
My grandmother kisses as if history
never ended, as if somewhere
a body is still
falling apart.

**Related Resource**

Vietnamese child refugees.

Records of the Office of the Chief Signal Officer, *Vietnamese Children Outside the Viet Huong Refugee Center*, 1972. Photograph, National Archives.

# One Nation Out of Many

## Activities

1. **Warm-up**: Closely look at the photograph of refugees fleeing Vietnam during the Vietnam War in 1972, and write down the details you see. What do you notice about the people in this photo?
2. **Before Reading the Poem**: Find a partner and share the details you wrote down. What story do you imagine for the people in this photo? What details make you think that?
3. **Reading the Poem**: Silently read "Kissing in Vietnamese" by Ocean Vuong. What do you notice about the poem? Note any words, phrases, or poetic structures that stand out to you and any questions you might have.
4. **Listening to the Poem**: Enlist two volunteers and listen as the poem is read aloud twice. What did you hear that you did not previously notice when you were reading the poem? Write down any additional words and phrases that stand out to you.
5. **Small Group Discussion**: Pick a phrase you found particularly compelling and use your body to create a tableau that illustrates this phrase. Take turns presenting the tableau to everyone. As each group presents, share the details you notice and the feelings you think are represented by the tableau.
6. **Large Group Discussion**: What emotions are represented in "Kissing in Vietnamese"? What do we learn from reading that we might not learn from our own experiences? Why might it be important to read about other people's experiences?
7. **Extension for Grades 7–8**: Use your imagination to write a poem or prose piece in the voice of one of the people in the photo. If you'd like, you can change the point of view—for example, write from the perspective of the photographer.
8. **Extension for Grades 9–12**: Read pages eleven and twelve of "After Action Report, 'The Battle of Hue, 2–26 February 1968,'" and write down the things that stand out to you, including words you don't know. Gather into small groups to share what you noticed, and modify your lists as you learn from each other. What details did you notice in the report? What is the writer's perspective? What kind of language is used in the report? How does the report's language and perspective differ from Vuong's? Why might that be? Write an essay examining how distance, diction, or imagery influence a reader's response to these two texts.

## More Context

### Poems

Explore more classic and contemporary poems about war, wartime, and veterans.

## Glossary Term

**Imagery** language in a poem that represents a sensory experience.

## "The Dream of Shoji"
*by Kimiko Hahn*

How to say *milk?* How to say *sand, snow, sow,*

*linen, cloud, cocoon,* or *albino?*
How to say *page* or *canvas* or *rice balls?*
Trying to recall Japanese, I blank out:

it's clear I know *forgetting*. Mother, tell me
what to call that paper screen that slides the interior in?

### Related Resource

Evening snow.

Suzuki Harunobu, 風流江戸八景 真乳山の暮雪 *(Evening Snow on Matsuchi Hill)*, ca. 1765–70. Polychrome woodblock print, Metropolitan Museum.

### Activities

1. **Warm-up**: Quickly go around the room and share a question about your heritage that you would like to ask a parent, relative, or guardian.
2. **Before Reading the Poem**: Look up the meaning of the word "shoji." Then look very closely at the image of the wood block print *Evening Snow on Matschi Hill* by Suzuki Harunobu. What are the various elements in the image? How are they composed? What is in the foreground? The background? What separates them? Share what you noticed with a partner.

3. **Reading the Poem**: Silently read "The Dream of Shoji" by Kimiko Hahn. What do you notice about the poem? Note any words, phrases, or poetic structures that stand out to you and any questions you might have.
4. **Listening to the Poem**: Enlist two volunteers and listen as the poem is read aloud twice. What did you hear that you did not previously notice when you were reading the poem? Write down any additional words and phrases that stand out to you.
5. **Small Group Discussion**: Share what you noticed in the poem. Are the composition of the poem and the image of the wood block print similar in any way? How are they different?
6. **Large Group Discussion**: Why do you think the speaker in the poem asks her mother "what to call that paper screen that slides from the interior in"? Might the shoji screen be a metaphor for something deeper?
7. **Extension for Grades 7–8**: Ask your parent, relative, or guardian the question about your heritage you mentioned in the warm-up activity. Record their response and ask follow-up questions. Write a summary and be prepared to present it to the group.
8. **Extension for Grades 9–12**: Write a poem in which you ask your parent, relative, or guardian the question you mentioned in the warm-up activity. Your poem should include the question, the person's answer, and one or two metaphors to deepen the reader's understanding of your exchange.

## More Context

### Video

In this video from a 2014 Chancellor Conversation, the poet Arthur Sze discusses his work as a translator and "how important and crucial translation is in the forming of our poetics and our own evolution and journey as poets." Watch the video.

## Glossary Term

**Translation** the art of transferring meaning from one language to another.

## "Red Brocade"

*by Naomi Shihab Nye*

The Arabs used to say,
When a stranger appears at your door,
feed him for three days
before asking who he is,
where he's come from,
where he's headed.
That way, he'll have strength
enough to answer.
Or, by then you'll be
such good friends
you don't care.

Let's go back to that.
Rice? Pine nuts?
Here, take the red brocade pillow.
My child will serve water
to your horse.

No, I was not busy when you came!
I was not preparing to be busy.
That's the armor everyone put on
to pretend they had a purpose
in the world.

I refuse to be claimed.
Your plate is waiting.
We will snip fresh mint
into your tea.

## Related Resource

Mint tea.

Chris Blackhead, *Mint Tea in Isfahan (Iran)*, 2014. Photograph, Flickr.

## Activities

1. **Warm-up**: Write a sentence about a time you felt very welcomed by someone.
2. **Before Reading the Poem**: Join with a partner and share answers to the following questions: How does your culture or family treat strangers? How does your culture treat close family members or friends? How is this the same or different? Why?
3. **Reading the Poem**: Silently read "Red Brocade" by Naomi Shihab Nye. What do you notice about the poem? Note any words, phrases, or poetic structures that stand out to you and any questions you might have.
4. **Listening to the Poem**: Enlist two volunteers and listen as the poem is read aloud twice. What did you hear that you did not previously notice when you were reading the poem? Write down any additional words and phrases that stand out to you.
5. **Small Group Discussion**: Share what you noticed in the poem with a small group, recalling the discussion from the beginning of this lesson. How does the speaker treat strangers? What might this imply about the speaker's culture?

6. **Large Group Discussion**: Reread the last two stanzas in the poem. What argument is the speaker making? Why? How is the speaker refusing to be "claimed"?
7. **Extension for Grades 7–8**: Think back to the discussion at the beginning of these activities. Write a poem that explores how your culture or family views treating others, or write one about another important aspect of your culture.
8. **Extension for Grades 9–12**: Think back to the discussion at the beginning of this lesson. Interview a friend or neighbor and ask them the same questions: How does your culture or family treat strangers? How does your culture treat close family members or friends? Then think about how this is similar to or different from your own culture. Why? Share your interview with the group, highlighting the similarities and differences. Be sure to ask permission before you share.

## More Context

### Video

In this video from the 2015 National Book Festival, Naomi Shihab Nye talks about the themes she finds herself returning to in her poetry, as well as the poet's civic responsibility "to continue to encourage a sense of civility among us and a sense of curiosity about one another's lives." Watch it here.

## Glossary Term

**Speaker** the voice of a poem, similar to a narrator in fiction.

## "Senior Discount"
### by Ali Liebegott

I want to grow old with you.
*Old, old.*

So old we pad through the supermarket
using the shopping cart as a cane that steadies us.

I'll wait at register two in my green sweater
with threadbare elbows, smiling
because you've forgotten the bag of day-old pastries.

The cashier will tell me a joke about barbers as I wait.
He repeats the first line three times
but the only word I understand is *barber*.

Over the years we've caught inklings
of our shrinking frames and hunched spines.

You're a little confused
looking for me at the wrong register with a bag
of almost-stale croissants clenched in your hand.

The first time I held your hand it felt enormous in my own.
*Sasquatch*, I teased you, a million years ago.

*Over here*, I yell, but not in a mad way.

We're laughing.
You have a bright yellow pin on your coat that says, *Shalom!*

*Senior Discount*, you say.
But the cashier already knows us.
We're everyone's favorite customers.

### Related Resource

Music video for "First Day of My Life" by Bright Eyes.

Saddle Creek Records, "Bright Eyes—First Day of My Life [Official Music Video]" 2006. Screenshot, YouTube.

## Activities

1. **Warm-up**: What does it mean to be old? Write about what you think your life would be like, including what you would do every day.
2. **Before Reading the Poem**: Closely watch the video for the song, "First Day of My Life" by Bright Eyes. What stands out to you? Why? Watch the video again. Who do you see? What's happening in the video? How do you know? Who do you see?
3. **Reading the Poem**: Silently read "Senior Discount" by Ali Liebegott. What do you notice about the poem? Note any words, phrases, or poetic structures that stand out to you and any questions you might have.
4. **Listening to the Poem**: Listen as Ali Liebegott reads her poem twice. What did you hear that you did not previously notice when you were reading the poem? Write down any additional words and phrases that stand out to you.
5. **Small Group Discussion**: Share what you noticed in the poem with your partner and another pair of students. How does the poet describe old age? How does this compare or contrast with your group's thoughts about old age from the warm-up activity?
6. **Large Group Discussion**: What is the significance of the title? How might the poem change with a different title? How is love expressed in the poem? Think back to the video you watched. What would it mean if the couple in the poem was LGBTQ+? Would anything change? Why or why not?
7. **Extension for Grades 7–8**: Write an imaginary journal or diary entry by you at an age you consider to be old. Draw from your writing during the warm-up, and include as many details as possible.
8. **Extension for Grades 9–12**: In small groups, write a script for an interview you would like to conduct with an elder about growing old. What advice would you ask for? Practice interviewing members of your group with this script, then interview elders you know, or coordinate with a local assisted living facility to arrange virtual or in-person interviews with a few elders. Present your findings to other members in your group. Be sure to ask permission before you share.

## More Context

### Biography

Ali Liebegott is a poet, novelist, and screenwriter. She is the author of the novel-in-verse, *The Summer of Dead Birds, 2013* (Amethyst Editions, 2019), the novels *Cha-Ching!* (City Lights, 2013), *The IHOP Papers* (Carroll & Graf, 2007), and *The Beautifully Worthless* (Suspect Thoughts, 2005). Her honors include two Lambda Literary Awards in Lesbian Debut Fiction and Lesbian Fiction, as well as a poetry fellowship from the New York Foundation of the Arts. She received a Peabody Award for her work as a writer for the TV show *Transparent*. She lives in Los Angeles, California.

### Glossary Term

**Couplet** a two-line stanza, or two successive lines of verse, rhymed or unrhymed.

## "Girls on the Town, 1946"
*by Rita Dove*

[Elvira H. D., 1924–2019]

You love a red lip. The dimples are
extra currency, though you take care to keep
    powder from caking those charmed valleys.
    Mascara: check. Blush? Oh, yes.
And a hat is never wrong
except evenings in the clubs: there
    a deeper ruby and smoldering eye
will do the trick, with tiny embellishments—
a ribbon or jewel, perhaps a flower—
if one is feeling especially flirty or sad.

Until Rosie fired up her rivets, flaunting
was a male prerogative; now, you and your girls
    have lacquered up and pinned on your tailfeathers,
    fit to sally forth and trample each plopped heart
    quivering at the tips of your patent-leather
Mary Janes. This is the only power you hold onto,
    ripped from the dreams none of you believe
are worth the telling. Instead of mumbling,
    why not decorate? Even in dim light
how you glister, sloe-eyed, your smile in flames.

**Related Resource**

"Rosie the Riveter" poster.

War Production Co-ordinating Committee, United States Creator. *We Can Do It!*, 1942–43. Poster, World Digital Library.

## Activities

1. **Warm-up**: What is beauty? Join with a peer or small group and discuss how beauty is important today.
2. **Before Reading the Poem**: Look closely at the poster of "Rosie the Riveter." What stands out to you in this poster? Why? What might this poster be advertising? Who might be the audience for this poster? Why?
3. **Reading the Poem**: Silently read "Girls On the Town, 1946" by Rita Dove. What do you notice about the poem? Note any words, phrases, or poetic structures that stand out to you and any questions you might have.
4. **Listening to the Poem**: Enlist two volunteers and listen as the poem is read aloud twice. What did you hear that you did not previously notice when you were reading the poem? Write down any additional words and phrases that stand out to you.
5. **Small Group Discussion**: Share what you noticed about the poem with a small group. Based on this poem and your earlier activities, how does the person in the first stanza feel about beauty? How does this compare to what you shared about beauty at the beginning of this lesson? What "currency" does beauty hold today?
6. **Large Group Discussion**: How does the second stanza compare to the first? How might "Rosie the Riveter" be related to the poem? What comparisons can you draw?

7. **Extension for Grades 7–8**: Continue reading more women poets. Choose a poet to read and explore. With a group, present what you learned about your selected poet and share a poem by that poet.
8. **Extension for Grades 9–12**: Continue reading more women poets. Choose one or more poets to read. Write your own poem that honors Women's History Month and a woman who is meaningful to you. With your group, create an anthology of these poems.

## More Context

### Article

"'Rosie the Riveter' was an iconic poster of a female factory worker flexing her muscle, exhorting other women to join the World War II effort with the declaration, "We Can Do It!" Mae Krier, born in 1926, the original Rosie the Riveter, worked at Boeing aircraft, producing B-17s and B-29s for the war effort from 1943 to 1945 in Seattle. Read more.

### Glossary Term

**Stanza** a grouping of lines that forms the main unit in a poem.

## "Haircut"

*by Elizabeth Alexander*

I get off the IRT in front of the Schomburg Center for Research in Black Culture after riding an early Amtrak from Philly to get a hair cut at what used to be the Harlem "Y" barbershop. It gets me in at ten to ten. Waiting, I eat fish cakes at the Pam Pam and listen to the ladies call out orders: bacon-biscuit twice, scrambled scrambled fried, over easy, grits, country sausage on the side. Hugh is late. He shampoos me, says "I can't remember, Girlfriend, are you tender-headed?" From the chair I notice the mural behind me in the mirror. I know those overlapped sepia shadows, a Renaissance rainforest, Aaron Douglas! Hugh tells me he didn't use primer and the chlorine eats the colors every day. He clips and combs and I tell him how my favorite Douglas is called "Building More Stately Mansions," and he tells me how fly I'd look in a Salt 'n' Pepa 'do, how he trained in Japan.

Clip clip, clip clip. I imagine a whoosh each time my hair lands on the floor and the noises of small brown mammals. I remember, my father! He used to get his hair cut here, learned to swim in the caustic water, played pool and basketball. He cuts his own hair now. My grandfather worked seventy-five years in Harlem building more stately mansions. I was born two blocks away and then we moved.

None of that seems to relate to today. This is not my turf, despite the other grandfather and great-aunt who sewed hearts back into black chests after Saturday night stabbings on this exact corner, the great-uncle who made a mosaic down the street, both grandmothers. What am I always listening for in Harlem? A voice that says, "This is your place, too," as faintly as the shadows in the mural? The accents are unfamiliar; all my New York kin are dead. I never knew Fats Waller but what do I do with knowing he used to play with a ham and a bottle of gin atop his piano; never went to Olivia's House of Beauty but I know Olivia, who lives in St. Thomas, now, and who exactly am I, anyway, finding myself in these ghostly, Douglas shadows while real ghosts walk around me, talk about my stuff in the subway, yell at me not to butt the line, beg me, beg me, for my money?

What is black culture? I read the writing on the wall on the side of the "Y" as I always have: "Harlem Plays the Best Ball in the World." I look in the mirror and see my face in the mural with a new haircut. I am a New York girl; I am a New York woman; I am a flygirl with a new hair cut in New York City in a mural that is dying every day.

# One Nation Out of Many

## Related Resource

Painting of a musician.

Aaron Douglas, *Aspects of Negro Life: Song of the Towers*, 1934. Oil on canvas, The New York Public Library, Schomburg Center for Research in Black Culture.

## Activities

1. **Warm-up**: Look carefully at the painting *Aspects of Negro Life: Song of the Towers* by Aaron Douglas, and write down as many things you notice as you can in two minutes.
2. **Before Reading the Poem**: Look at the way "Haircut" appears on the page. Does it look like other poems you have read? In what ways is it similar? In what ways is it different? Review the term "prose poem."
3. **Reading the Poem**: Silently read "Haircut" by Elizabeth Alexander. What do you notice about the poem? Note any words, phrases, or poetic structures that stand out to you and any questions you might have.
4. **Listening to the Poem**: Enlist two volunteers and listen as the poem is read aloud twice. What did you hear that you did not previously notice when you were reading the poem? Write down any additional words and phrases that stand out to you.
5. **Small Group Discussion**: Although the particular painting you observed is not the one referenced in the poem, it represents the painter's style. Does it relate to "Haircut" in any way? If so, how?
6. **Large Group Discussion**: What is Elizabeth Alexander saying about the speaker of the poem's culture and how they fit within it? What details from the poem tell you this?
7. **Extension for Grades 7–8**: Make a list of places you haven't been to recently. Write a prose poem about visiting one of these places and what it might say to you. Describe how it looks, sounds, and smells, and include dialogue.

8. **Extension for Grades 9–12**: The speaker of the poem says, "I remember, my father!" Interview a family member or respected elder about somewhere they visited regularly when they were young. Ask how the place looked, sounded, and smelled. What did they do there and who did they talk to? Write a prose poem about visiting that place. What would you ask it? What would it say?

## More Context

### Video

In a video from the Rhode Island School of Design Museum about Aaron Douglas's painting, *Building More Stately Mansions*, the curators ask, "Who does the work of building a great society? Who gets credited and remembered by history?"

## Glossary Term

**Prose poem** a poem that lacks the line breaks traditionally associated with poetry.

## "Crossing"
*by Jericho Brown*

The water is one thing, and one thing for miles.
The water is one thing, making this bridge
Built over the water another. Walk it
Early, walk it back when the day goes dim, everyone
Rising just to find a way toward rest again.
We work, start on one side of the day
Like a planet's only sun, our eyes straight
Until the flame sinks. The flame sinks. Thank God
I'm different. I've figured and counted. I'm not crossing
To cross back. I'm set
On something vast. It reaches
Long as the sea. I'm more than a conqueror, bigger
Than bravery. I don't march. I'm the one who leaps.

## Related Resource

The Edmund Pettus Bridge crossing.

U.S. National Park Service, *First of the Selma to Montgomery Marches, Carter G. Woodson Home National Historic Site, 1965*. Photograph, National Park Service Gallery.

## Activities

1. **Warm-up**: In your life, how do you use your voice to protest? Write down times you have told people you disagreed with them.
2. **Before Reading the Poem**: Look carefully at the photograph *First of the Selma to Montgomery Marches, Carter G. Woodson Home National Historic Site, 1965*, taken during the Edmund Pettus Bridge crossing on March 7, 1965. What do you notice? Look again. What else do you see?

3. **Reading the Poem**: Silently read "Crossing" by Jericho Brown. What do you notice about the poem? Note any words, phrases, or poetic structures that stand out to you and any questions you might have.
4. **Listening to the Poem**: Enlist two volunteers and listen as the poem is read aloud twice. What did you hear that you did not previously notice when you were reading the poem? Write down any additional words and phrases that stand out to you.
5. **Small Group Discussion**: (Educators, you may wish to share more context about the photograph.) Share what you noticed in the poem with a small group. Based on the details you just shared, how might the image from activity two or your prior knowledge of the Edmund Pettus Bridge crossing relate to the poem? How is the poem similar to or different from the photograph? Why?
6. **Large Group Discussion**: What do you think of the line, "I don't march. I'm the one who leaps"? What is the difference between leaping and marching? What does this reveal about the speaker of the poem?
7. **Extension for Grades 7–8**: Watch a video about Dr. Martin Luther King's granddaughter discussing the importance of creating her own legacy. Create a poem, speech, drawing, dance, or skit in which you forge your own legacy. Perform your piece in front of your peers.
8. **Extension for Grades 9–12**: Reread the poem. Think about the final six lines and write an essay, poem, or speech that answers the following questions: How and why is the speaker of the poem different? How are you different? What is your legacy? Share your piece.

## More Context

### About the Resource

The description of the Edmund Pettus Bridge crossing reads,

> A peaceful civil rights demonstration that included a march across the Edmund Pettus Bridge would eventually become known as "Bloody Sunday" by the African American community. On March 7, 1965, civil rights demonstrators attempting to march to the state capital of Montgomery began crossing the Edmund Pettus Bridge. Due to the bridge's construction, demonstrators had no idea their exit was blocked by police officers on the east side of the bridge. However, even after reaching the top of the bridge and seeing the police officers, demonstrators continued marching without stopping. They were attacked and beaten by police as they tried to peacefully continue their march across the bridge. Televised images of the brutal attack presented international and national audiences with horrifying images of marchers left bloodied and severely injured, including that of Amelia Boynton, who was beaten unconscious and left

 lying on the road. Her photograph was shown on front pages of newspapers and news magazines around the world. Since 1965, many marches have commemorated these events, including a 30th anniversary event in 1995, the 40th reunion in 2005 when over 10,000 people gathered again to march across the bridge and again in 2015 on the 50th anniversary when President Barack Obama, former President George W. Bush and Amelia Boynton Robinson led the march across the bridge.

## Glossary Term

**Voice** an expression denoting the comprehensive style of a speaker adopted by the author in a poem.

## "Maps"
### by Yesenia Montilla

*for Marcelo*

Some maps have blue borders
like the blue of your name
or the tributary lacing of
veins running through your
father's hands. & how the last
time I saw you, you held
me for so long I saw whole
lifetimes flooding by me
small tentacles reaching
for both our faces. I wish
maps would be without
borders & that we belonged
to no one & to everyone
at once, what a world that
would be. Or not a world
maybe we would call it
something more intrinsic
like forgiving or something
simplistic like river or dirt.
& if I were to see you
tomorrow & everyone you
came from had disappeared
I would weep with you & drown
out any black lines that this
earth allowed us to give it—
because what is a map but
a useless prison? We are all
so lost & no naming of blank
spaces can save us. & what
is a map but the delusion of
safety? The line drawn is always
in the sand & folds on itself
before we're done making it.
& that line, there, south of
el rio, how it dares to cover
up the bodies, as though we
would forget who died there
& for what? As if we could
forget that if you spin a globe
& stop it with your finger
you'll land it on top of someone
living, someone who was not
expecting to be crushed by thirst—

## Related Resource

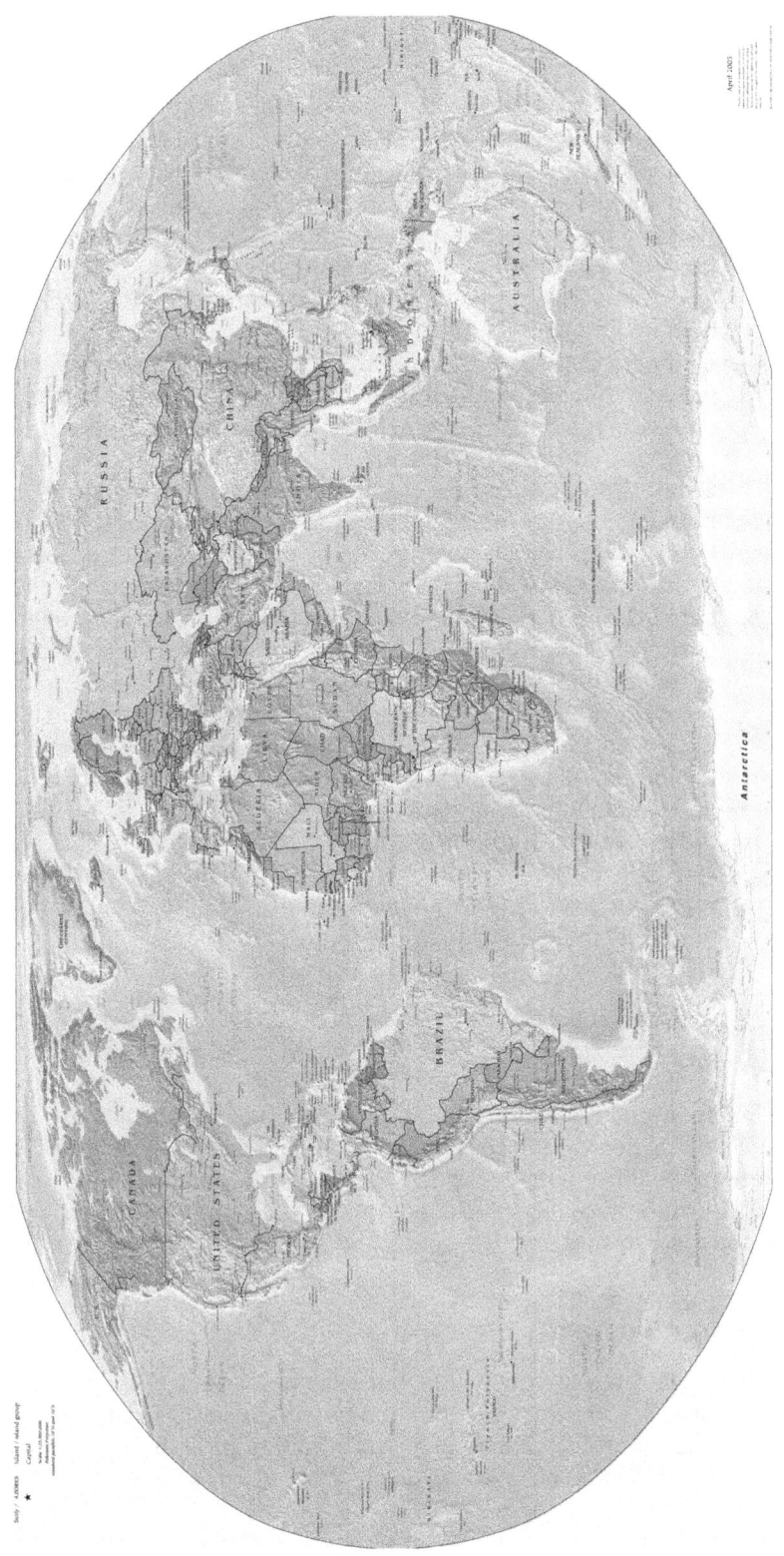

World map.
Central Intelligence Agency, *World Map*, 2005. Digital image, Wikimedia Commons.

## Activities

1. **Warm-up**: Look at the world map and write down the objective details you notice about the map. For example, what colors and shapes does the mapmaker use to represent mountains, rivers, and countries?
2. **Before Reading the Poem**: Share your notes with a partner. Was it easy or difficult to describe the map without making inferences? Why or why not?
3. **Reading the Poem**: Silently read "Maps" by Yesenia Montilla. What do you notice about the poem? Note any words, phrases, or poetic structures that stand out to you and any questions you might have.

4. **Listening to the Poem**: Listen twice to Yesenia Montilla reading her poem. What did you hear that you did not previously notice when you were reading the poem? Write down any additional words and phrases that stand out to you.
5. **Small Group Discussion**: Recall the lines that stood out to you in the poem by saying them aloud in a small group. Based on the lines, how does the poem relate to the details you noticed in the world map? How does the speaker in the poem feel about maps?
6. **Large Group Discussion**: What does the speaker in the poem want to do with maps? Why do they feel that way? Do you agree or disagree with the speaker's perspective? Use evidence from the poem to support your answers.
7. **Extension for Grades 7–8**: Write a poem dedicated to a friend or loved one telling them everything you wish to do for them. Share your poem with a partner.
8. **Extension for Grades 9–12**: Read the glossary entry for "ekphrasis." How is "Maps" part of a tradition of using ekphrasis to interrogate or interpret? Write your own ekphrasis of a cultural image you'd like to interrogate or interpret.

## More Context

### Article

In an interview with PBS, Marcelo Hernandez Castillo (to whom "Maps" Is dedicated), says English fluency was "a way to kind of offset any questions or any suspicions about my documentation status." Read more about Castillo's experience as a migrant and how it has influenced his poetry.

### Glossary Term

**Ekphrasis**  the use of vivid language to describe or respond to a work of visual art. In the nineteenth and twentieth centuries, the term took on a new purpose, exchanging the tradition of elaborate description for interpretation or interrogation.

## "Perhaps the World Ends Here"
*by Joy Harjo*

The world begins at a kitchen table. No matter what, we must eat to live.

The gifts of earth are brought and prepared, set on the table. So it has been since creation, and it will go on.

We chase chickens or dogs away from it. Babies teethe at the corners. They scrape their knees under it.

It is here that children are given instructions on what it means to be human. We make men at it, we make women.

At this table we gossip, recall enemies and the ghosts of lovers.

Our dreams drink coffee with us as they put their arms around our children. They laugh with us at our poor falling-down selves and as we put ourselves back together once again at the table.

This table has been a house in the rain, an umbrella in the sun.

Wars have begun and ended at this table. It is a place to hide in the shadow of terror. A place to celebrate the terrible victory.

We have given birth on this table, and have prepared our parents for burial here.

At this table we sing with joy, with sorrow. We pray of suffering and remorse. We give thanks.

Perhaps the world will end at the kitchen table, while we are laughing and crying, eating of the last sweet bite.

## Related Resource

Photograph of a couple eating dinner.

Gordon Parks, *Washington, D.C. Elderly Couple Eating Dinner at Their Home on Lamont Street, N.W.*, 1942. Photograph, Library of Congress.

## Activities

1. **Warm-up**: Look at the image of the elderly couple eating dinner in 1942 What do you see? Look again. What else do you notice?
2. **Before Reading the Poem**: With a partner, discuss what you noticed in the photo. Do you relate to the image? Why or why not? If you're comfortable, share who you eat with and what it's like.
3. **Reading the Poem**: Silently read "Perhaps the World Ends Here" by Joy Harjo. What do you notice about the poem? Note any words, phrases, or poetic structures that stand out to you and any questions you might have.
4. **Listening to the Poem**: Enlist two volunteers and listen as the poem is read aloud twice. What did you hear that you did not previously notice when you were reading the poem? Write down any additional words and phrases that stand out to you.
5. **Small Group Discussion**: Share what you noticed in the poem with a small group. Based on the discussion from the beginning of these activities and what you just shared with your small group, what is the role of the kitchen table? Why? What rituals are performed at the table?
6. **Large Group Discussion**: Reread the line: "The world begins at a kitchen table. No matter what, we must eat to live." What might the significance of this line be? What is your favorite image or ritual in the poem? Why?

7. **Extension for Grades 7–8**: Use the photograph you viewed during the warm-up or the imagery in the poem to write an origin story of the table present. How did this table come to be? What materials is it made of? How did the table make its way to the family in the poem or in the photograph?
8. **Extension for Grades 9–12**: Compare and contrast the table in the photo and the poem. How do your personal rituals compare and contrast to those in the poem? Write a personal essay that is poetic. Try adding line breaks to the essay like Harjo does in this poem.

## More Context

### Interview

In a 2019 interview with Joy Harjo, she says,

> I see and hear the presence of generations making poetry through the many cultures that express America. They range from ceremonial orality which might occur from spoken word to European fixed forms; to the many classic traditions that occur in all cultures, including theoretical abstract forms that find resonance on the page or in image.

## Glossary Term

**Caesura** a pause for a beat in the rhythm of a verse, often indicated by a line break or by punctuation.

## "Survival Guide"
*by Joy Ladin*

No matter how old you are,
it helps to be young
when you're coming to life,

to be unfinished, a mysterious statement,
a journey from star to star.
So break out a box of Crayolas

and draw your family
looking uncomfortably away
from the you you've exchanged

for the mannequin
they named. You should
help clean up, but you're so busy being afraid

to love or not
you're missing the fun of clothing yourself
in the embarrassment of life.

Frost your lids with midnight;
lid your heart with frost;
rub them all over, the hormones that regulate

the production of love
from karmic garbage dumps.
Turn yourself into

the real you
you can only discover
by being other.

Voila! You're free.
Learn to love the awkward silence
you are going to be.

# One Nation Out of Many

## Related Resource

Painting of a woman in a mirror.

Berthe Morisot, *The Psyche Mirror*, 1876. Painting, Thyssen-Bornemisza Museum, Madrid.

## Activities

1. **Warm-up**: What does it mean to survive? If you feel comfortable, share your response with a peer.
2. **Before Reading the Poem**: Discuss with a partner: If you were going to create a survival guide for other people your age, what three things might you include? Why?
3. **Reading the Poem**: Silently read "Survival Guide" by Joy Ladin. What do you notice about the poem? Note any words, phrases, or poetic structures that stand out to you and any questions you might have.
4. **Listening to the Poem**: Enlist two volunteers and listen as the poem is read aloud twice. What did you hear that you did not previously notice when you were reading the poem? Write down any additional words and phrases that stand out to you.
5. **Small Group Discussion**: Share what you noticed in the poem with a small group of students. Based on the details you just shared with your small group and your discussions during the warm-up and activity two, how is this poem a survival guide? What advice does the speaker of the poem give for survival?
6. **Large Group Discussion**: In the poem, what imagery feels the most powerful? Discuss the significance of these lines: "Learn to love/ the awkward silence you are going to be," and "Turn yourself into/ the real you/you can only discover by being other"?
7. **Extension for Grades 7–8**: Think back to what you discussed at the beginning of the group activities. Write a letter to your future self. What advice would you give yourself about survival?

8. **Extension for Grades 9–12**: Read Ladin's article on identity and language, "I Am Not Not Me: Unmaking and Remaking the Language of the Self." What language do you use to describe yourself? Why? How does language connect to identity? Write a response to Ladin's article about your own relationship to language and identity.

## More Context

### Glossary Resource

The power of language to shape our perceptions of other people is immense. Precise use of terms in regard to gender and sexual orientation can have a significant impact on demystifying many of the misperceptions associated with these concepts. However, the vocabulary of both continues to evolve, and there is not universal agreement about the definitions of many terms. A good best practice is to ask people what the words they use to describe themselves mean for them and how they would like you to use language when talking with or about them.

Browse the PFLAG National Glossary of Terms.

### Glossary Term

**Meter** the measured pattern of rhythmic accents in a line of verse.

# 2 The Pursuit of Equality

## Introduction

As educators, you play a key role in guiding conversations about equity, and it's helpful to approach them with a focus on sensitivity, equality, and inclusion. Whereas the last chapter mapped culture and legacy, this chapter covers documentation, understanding, and history based on lived experiences.

It's important to be prepared for deep conversation. According to "Fostering Civil Discourse: Difficult Classroom Conversations in a Diverse Democracy" by Facing History & Ourselves, this means having some strategies ready for guiding discussions, handling sensitive topics gently, addressing unplanned moments, generating reflection questions, and encouraging students to think critically. When you're well prepared, you create a space where participants feel confident to explore and discuss complex issues.

Having the right tools to navigate these discussions effectively is key and ensures that all voices are respected and heard. Reviewing the poems, activities, and resources beforehand and thinking about them in relation to your group, school, or greater community can help you identify any points that may require extra sensitivity and attention. Understanding changing standards for teaching in your area is essential, as is adhering to local regulations.

Hess and McAvoy state the following in *The Political Classroom: Evidence and Ethics in Democratic Education*:

> [H]igh school students who engaged in rigorous political discussions in their social studies classes were more likely after graduating to be politically engaged, listen to those with different perspectives than them, and also pay attention to the news than students who did not have these discussions.
>
> (Routledge, 2015)

Teaching poetry can inform critical thinking and social emotional skills in lasting and vital ways. Despite the challenges of surfacing topical issues, by braving sensitive territory, you're providing insight that participants may not receive in other areas of study.

## "Lesson VIII: Map of North America"
### by Elizabeth Bradfield

> —*redacted from* Smith's Quarto, or Second Book in Geography, 1848, p. 17

    division

    division

            general divisions

      opposite

cluster    clusters    What considerable number

    Where is

          Where is Cape Farewell?

What sound leads into      the largest

    What  What  What  What

Boundaries  Bound United    Bound

    the   New   ?   Bound   possessions?

    What  What  What  What

prevails

    What  What  What  What

races  What   race?

## Related Resources

Map of North America.

Roswell Chamberlain Smith, "Page 16," *Smith's Quarto, or Second Book in Geography. A Concise and Practical System of Geography*, 1848a. Book, Cady & Burgess.

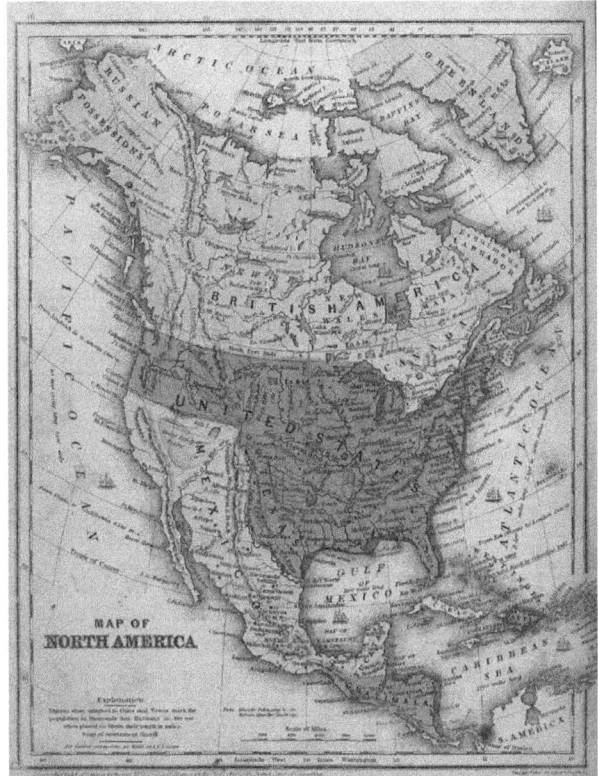

Notes on divisions in the map.

Roswell Chamberlain Smith, "Page 17," *Smith's Quarto, or Second Book in Geography. A Concise and Practical System of Geography*, 1848b. Book, Cady & Burgess.

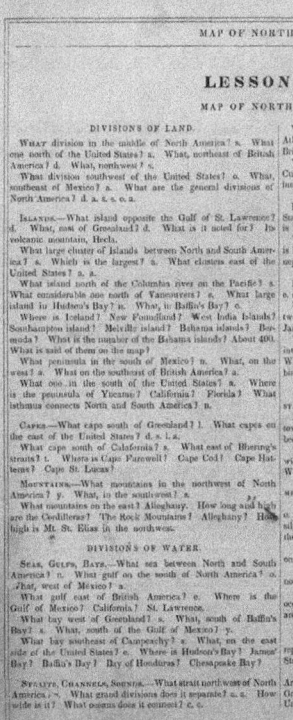

## Activities

1. **Warm-up:** Why do we use maps? What maps do you use? Why?
2. **Before Reading the Poem:** Look carefully at the map of North America. What do you notice? Why might this map have been created? Who might the audience be? Look at the second image of the accompanying Lesson VIII: Map of North America. What do you notice about this image? How does it compare to the map? What do you wonder about the two images?
3. **Reading the Poem:** Silently read "Lesson VIII: Map of North America" by Elizabeth Bradfield. What do you notice about the poem? Note any words, phrases, or poetic structures that stand out to you and any questions you might have.
4. **Listening to the Poem:** Enlist two volunteers and listen as the poem is read aloud twice. What did you hear that you did not previously notice when you were reading the poem? Write down any additional words and phrases that stand out to you.
5. **Small Group Discussion:** Share what you noticed in the poem with a small group. Based on the details you just shared, how might the images from the activity relate to the poem? Why?
6. **Large Group Discussion:** Review the term "erasure." What do you think is the significance of the lines "Boundaries Bound United Bound/the New? Bound possessions?" How does what you have learned about erasure poetry affect or not affect the way that you read the poem?
7. **Extension for Grades 7–8:** Choose another of Elizabeth Bradfield's poems to read. Write an essay that compares and contrasts the chosen poem with "Lesson VIII: Map of North America." Explore structure and theme.
8. **Extension for Grades 9–12:** With a partner, read Yesenia Montilla's poem "Maps." Then discuss how the two poems might act as visual maps. Create a map for each poem. What would be represented in each? What would be left out? Why? Present your maps to your group.

## More Context

### Online Tool: Emerge

Explore Emerge, an online tool that enables students to make, save, and send erasure poems by selecting words to surface from a source text. This tool is presented in partnership with the Wick Poetry Center at Kent State University and features source texts related to democracy.

## Glossary Term

**Erasure** a form of found poetry wherein a poet takes an existing text and erases, blacks out, or otherwise obscures a large portion of the text, creating a wholly new work from what remains.

## "They Don't Love You Like I Love You"
*by Natalie Diaz*

My mother said this to me
long before Beyoncé lifted the lyrics
from the Yeah Yeah Yeahs,

and what my mother meant by
*Don't stray* was that she knew
all about it—the way it feels to need

someone to love you, someone
not *your kind*, someone white,
some one some many who live

because so many of mine
have not, and further, live on top of
those of ours who don't.

*I'll say, say, say,*
*I'll say, say, say,*
What is the United States if not a clot

of clouds? If not spilled milk? Or blood?
If not the place we once were
in the millions? America is *Maps*—

Maps are ghosts: white and
layered with people and places I see through.
My mother has always known best,

knew that I'd been begging for them,
to lay my face against their white
laps, to be held in something more

than the loud light of their projectors
as they flicker themselves—sepia
or blue—all over my body.

All this time,
I thought my mother said, *Wait*,
as in, *Give them a little more time*

*to know your worth*,
when really, she said, *Weight*,
meaning *heft*, preparing me

for the yoke of myself,
the beast of my country's burdens,
which is less worse than

my country's plow. Yes,
when my mother said,
*They don't love you like I love you*,

she meant,
*Natalie, that doesn't mean
you aren't good.*

\*The italicized words, with the exception of the final stanza, come from the Yeah Yeah Yeahs song "Maps."

## Related Resources

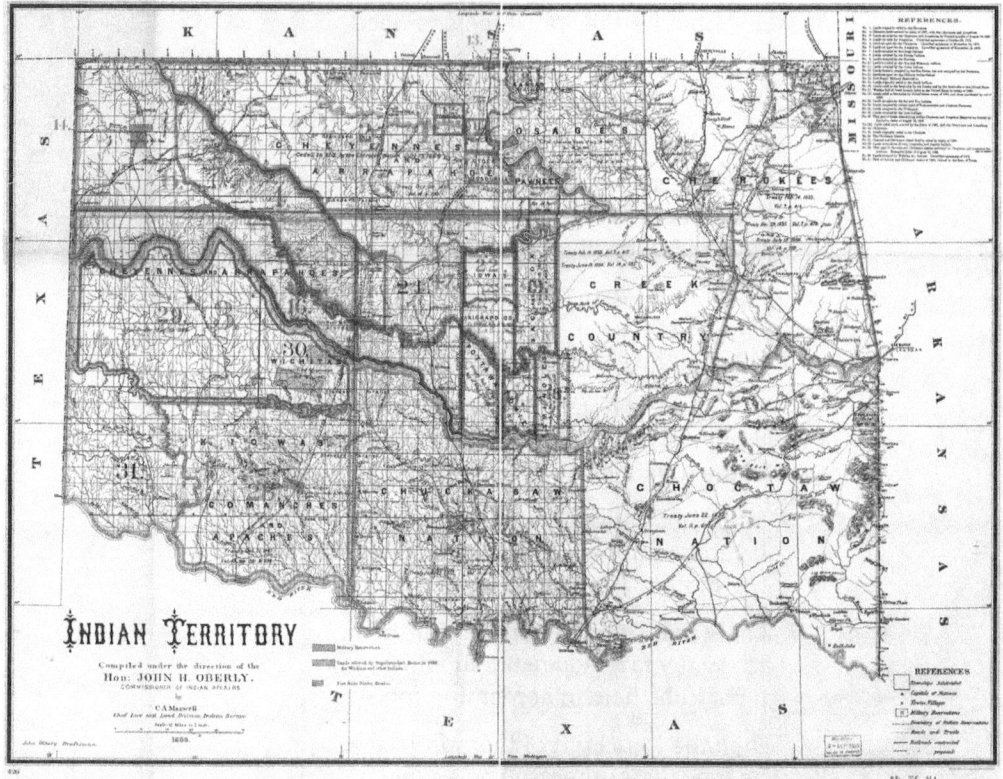

Indigenous territory, 1889.

Charles A Maxwell and United States Office of Indian Affairs, *Indian Territory: Compiled under the Direction of the Hon. John H. Oberly, Commissioner of Indian Affairs*, 1889. Map, Library of Congress.

The Pursuit of Equality

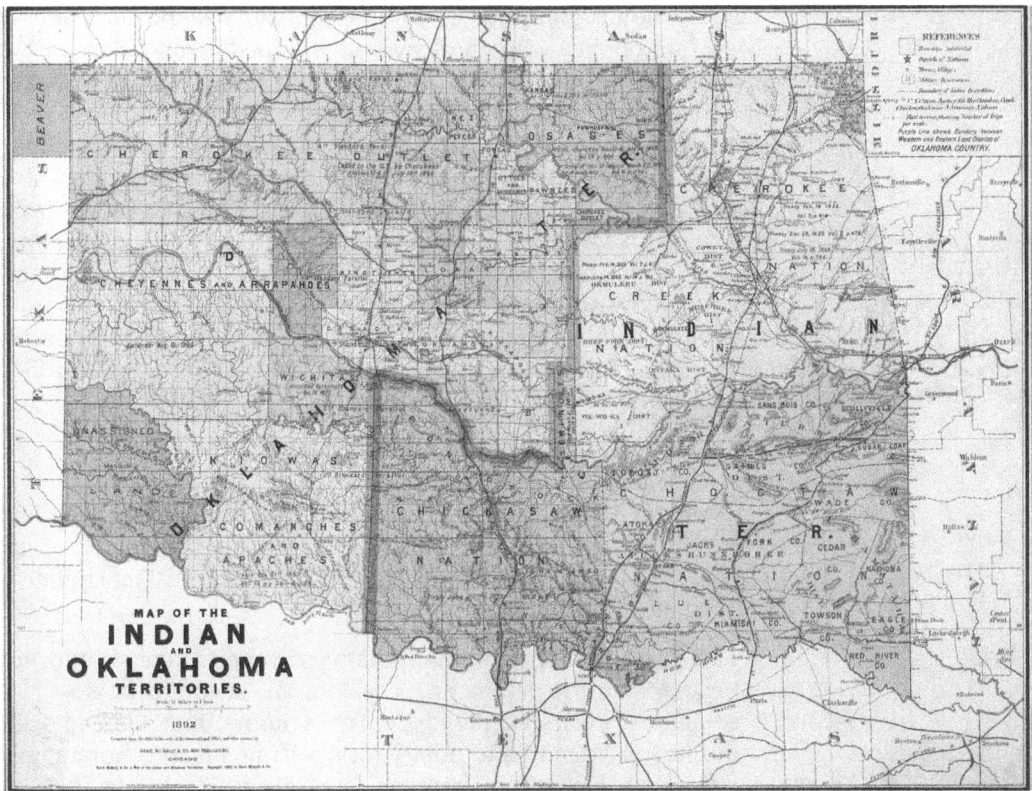

Indigenous and Oklahoma territories, 1892.

Rand McNally and Company, *Map of the Indian and Oklahoma Territories*, 1892. Map, Library of Congress.

## Activities

1. **Warm-up**: Compose a list that answers the following questions: What is the purpose of a map? Why do we use maps?
2. **Before Reading the Poem**: Look carefully at the first map from 1889. What stands out to you? Why? Look at the second map from 1892. What stands out to you in this map? Why? How are these two images connected? What has changed during the three years between them?
3. **Reading the Poem**: Silently read "They Don't Love You Like I Love You" by Natalie Diaz. What do you notice about the poem? Note any words, phrases, or poetic structures that stand out to you and any questions you might have.
4. **Listening to the Poem**: Watch Natalie Diaz read her poem twice. What did you hear that you did not previously notice when you were reading the poem? Write down any additional words and phrases that stand out to you.
5. **Small Group Discussion**: Share what you noticed in the poem with a small group. How would you describe the speaker of the poem? How would you describe the mother? What do the two want from each other?

6. **Large Group Discussion**: Reread the phrase, "America is *Maps*—// Maps are ghosts: white and/layered with people and places I see through." What might these lines mean? How do they compare to the maps and the list you made about the purpose of maps?
7. **Extension for Grades 7–8**: The poem was inspired by a song called "Maps" by the Yeah Yeah Yeahs. Watch the video of the song. Think about a song that means a lot to you. Drawing inspiration from Diaz's poem, write a poem that uses lines from your chosen song.
8. **Extension for Grades 9–12**: Research the poetic tradition of sampling. Following the form of a cento, write a love poem to someone or something built only out of lines from other books, poems, or songs. Use at least one line from "They Don't Love You Like I Love You."

## More Context

### Essay

In "A Poetry Portfolio: Featuring Five of Our Country's Finest Native Poets," Natalie Diaz writes,

> There is a reason why many natives come to poetry, and not because, as I've heard on occasion, we speak in poetry. Not because we were born with poetry in our mouths and eagles in our hearts. We come to poetry for the same reasons nonnatives come to poetry...it is a place to remember what has been done to us and to others, to remind those who have done those things to us, to challenge the world, to elegize our loved ones, and it's also a place to be hopeful and grateful—a space that simultaneously encompasses the past, present, and future.

## Glossary Term

**Cento** a form also known as a collage poem and composed entirely of lines from poems by other poets.

## "Declaration"
*by Tracy K. Smith*

*He has*

> *sent hither swarms of Officers to harass our people*

*He has plundered our—*

> *ravaged our—*
>
>> *destroyed the lives of our—*

*taking away our—*

> *abolishing our most valuable—*

*and altering fundamentally the Forms of our—*

*In every stage of these Oppressions We have Petitioned for Redress in the most humble terms:*

> *Our repeated*

*Petitions have been answered only by repeated injury.*

*We have reminded them of the circumstances of our emigration and settlement here.*

> *—taken Captive*
>
>> *on the high Seas*
>>
>>> *to bear—*

## Related Resource

Painting of the writing of the Declaration of Independence.

John Trumbull and the Illman Brothers, *The Declaration of Independence*, 1876. Engraving, Library of Congress.

## Activities

1. **Warm-up**: On a sticky note, write down what freedom means to you. When you finish, add your note to a shared space in the room.
2. **Before Reading the Poem**: Look carefully at the painting *The Declaration of Independence* by John Trumball. With a partner, discuss what is happening in the image. Look again. What else do you notice? What is going on in the room? Who is in the room? Who is absent from the room?
3. **Reading the Poem**: Silently read "Declaration" by Tracy K. Smith. What do you notice about the poem? Note any words, phrases, or poetic structures that stand out to you and any questions you might have.
4. **Listening to the Poem**: Enlist two volunteers and listen as the poem is read aloud twice. What did you hear that you did not previously notice when you were reading the poem? Write down any additional words and phrases that stand out to you.

5. **Small Group Discussion**: Share what you noticed in the poem with your partner and another pair of participants. Based on the details you shared, what connections can you make between the poem and the image? In what ways are they similar or different?
6. **Large Group Discussion**: Review the poetic term "erasure." How does it affect your reading to know that this poem is an erasure of the Declaration of Independence? Who is the "he" in the poem and what is his role? Who do you think is speaking in the poem, and how does it relate to the engraving? What is purposefully missing from the poem?
7. **Extension for Grades 7–8**: Using this version of the Declaration of Independence, try erasing words by shading or covering words that you want to remove. What new meaning did you create?
8. **Extension for Grades 9–12**: With your partner, take turns looking closely at the original Declaration of Independence and Smith's edits. Discuss how each of these edits could have changed the course of American history. Write your own version of the first two paragraphs, and write a paragraph explaining your decisions.

## More Context

### Interview

When she was appointed the twenty-second U.S. poet laureate, Tracy K. Smith spoke to the Academy of American Poets about the role of the poet in American culture. She said,

> I see the poet as someone who has made a commitment not just to self-expression, but to an active and eager listening to the world and the voices outside of the self. The poet is willing to be changed by the things that language can reveal—about who we are, how we live, what our impact upon the world and one another is.

### Glossary Term

**Political poetry** poetry that is related to activism, protest, and social concern, or that is commenting on social, political, or current events.

## "Dirt"
### by Kwame Dawes

> I got one part of it. Sell them watermelons and get me another part. Get Bernice to sell that piano and I'll have the third part.
> —August Wilson

We who gave, owned nothing,
learned the value of dirt, how
a man or a woman can stand
among the unruly growth,
look far into its limits,
a place of stone and entanglements,
and suddenly understand
the meaning of a name, a deed,
a currency of personhood.
Here, where we have labored
for another man's gain, if it is fine
to own dirt and stone, it is
fine to have a plot where
a body may be planted to rot.
We who have built only
that which others have owned
learn the ritual of trees,
the rites of fruit picked
and eaten, the pleasures
of ownership. We who
have fled with sword
at our backs know the things
they have stolen from us, and we
will walk naked and filthy
into the open field knowing
only that this piece of dirt,
this expanse of nothing,
is the earnest of our faith
in the idea of tomorrow.
We will sell our bones
for a piece of dirt,
we will build new tribes
and plant new seeds
and bury our bones in our dirt.

The Pursuit of Equality

## Related Resource

![Photograph of people planting sweet potatoes at Hopkinson's Plantation, 1862]

Photograph of people planting sweet potatoes.

Henry P. Moore, *Sweet Potato Planting, Hopkinson's Plantation*, 1862. Photograph, Library of Congress.

### Activities

1. **Warm-up**: Gather with a partner and take turns making an appropriate gesture with your body that you associate with the word "dirt." Why did you choose that gesture?
2. **Before Reading the Poem**: Carefully look at the photograph of people planting sweet potatoes. How are the people positioned? What can you learn from the positions of their bodies? With your partner, share what you've noticed and learned.
3. **Reading the Poem**: Silently read "Dirt" by Kwame Dawes. What do you notice about the poem? Note any words, phrases, or poetic structures that stand out to you and any questions you might have.
4. **Listening to the Poem**: Enlist two volunteers and listen as the poem is read aloud twice. What did you hear that you did not previously notice when you were reading the poem? Write down any additional words and phrases that stand out to you.

59

5. **Small Group Discussion**: What words, phrases, and poetic structures did you notice in the poem? How does the poem relate to the photograph? Does looking at the poem and photograph together help answer some of your questions? What questions remain?
6. **Large Group Discussion**: With a group, share what you discovered in your discussions and any remaining questions you have. Why is dirt important to the speaker in the poem?
7. **Extension for Grades 7–8**: Think about what you associated with the word "dirt" during the warm-up. Has it changed at all? Discuss the best things about dirt with your partner, and write a short poem about what you would do with a field of dirt. Review the term "consonance" and experiment with repeating sounds in your poem.

8. **Extension for Grades 9–12**: Read the first page of "The Agitation of Slavery," a political pamphlet from the pre–Civil War South. What is the pamphlet's argument for continuing slavery? How does this relate to Dawes's poem? In small groups, research and create a timeline of the movement for reparations.

## More Context

### Video

In "Writers Block: A Q&A with Kwame Dawes" with City of Asylum, Dawes says, "Ignorance, anxiety, joy, the lives of other people and the narratives of other people and trying to find the language to capture that—that's the drive. That's the thing that moves me." Watch the interview.

## Glossary Term

**Consonance** the repetition of similar consonant sounds.

The Pursuit of Equality

## "Making History"
### by Marilyn Nelson

*Blue and White Orlon Snowflake Sweater, Blue Snowpants, Red Galoshes*

—*Smoky Hill AFB, Kansas, 1955*

Somebody took a picture of a class
standing in line to get polio shots,
and published it in the *Weekly Reader*.
We stood like that today. And it did hurt.
Mrs. Liebel said we were Making History,
but all I did was sqwunch up my eyes and wince.
Making History takes more than standing in line
believing little white lies about pain.
Mama says First Negroes are History:
First Negro Telephone Operator,
First Negro Opera Singer At The Met,
First Negro Pilots, First Supreme Court Judge.
That lady in Montgomery just became a First
by sqwunching up her eyes and sitting there.

### Related Resource

Rosa Parks on a bus in Montgomery, Alabama.

*New York World–Telegram* and the *Sun Newspaper, Seating arrangements Mrs. Rosa Parks, 43, woman whose arrest on December 1st, 1955, touched off a year-long bus boycott by the Negro community here, gazes out of the window from a seat far forward in the bus she boarded here December 21st, as the boycott came to an end. Mrs. Parks was arrested originally when she sat in bus forward of white passengers*, 1956. Photograph, Library of Congress.

## Activities

1. **Warm-up**: Carefully look at the photograph of a woman on the bus, and write down what you see. Do you recognize anything about the picture? What details would you use to describe this photograph to another person?
2. **Before Reading the Poem**: Read the full title of the photograph. With a partner, discuss how the photo, taken a year after her arrest, might be different from the time when Parks was arrested. What do you think might be different? Why?
3. **Reading the Poem**: Silently read "Making History" by Marilyn Nelson. What do you notice about the poem? Note any words, phrases, or poetic structures that stand out to you and any questions you might have.
4. **Listening to the Poem**: Enlist two volunteers and listen as the poem is read aloud twice. What did you hear that you did not previously notice when you were reading the poem? Write down any additional words and phrases that stand out to you.
5. **Small Group Discussion**: Take turns sharing what you noticed in the poem with a small group. Based on the details you just shared, how does the poem relate to the photograph? In what ways is the speaker of the poem like Rosa Parks? How do you know?
6. **Large Group Discussion**: What is necessary to "make history" according to the speaker in the poem? What are the "little white lies?"
7. **Extension for Grades 7–8**: Review the definition of "persona poem." Explore the "Rosa Parks" collection of primary sources at the Library of Congress, and pick a photo that interests you. Write a persona poem from the point of view of someone or something in the photo. How does the person or object feel about the events happening around them or it? Is it new or has it happened before?
8. **Extension for Grades 9–12**: Learn about the long history of transportation activism in the United States by exploring this timeline. Research public transportation in your area. What kinds of transportation are available? How much does it cost? Does it serve all neighborhoods equally? In a small group, prepare a presentation to share your findings.

## More Context

### Documents

Explore the Library of Congress' "Rosa Parks" collection of primary documents covering her long career as a civil rights activist.

## Glossary Term

**Persona poem** a poem in which the poet assumes the voice of another person, fictional character, or identity.

# The Pursuit of Equality

## "Won't You Celebrate With Me"
*by Lucille Clifton*

won't you celebrate with me
what i have shaped into
a kind of life? i had no model.
born in babylon
both nonwhite and woman
what did i see to be except myself?
i made it up
here on this bridge between
starshine and clay,
my one hand holding tight
my other hand; come celebrate
with me that everyday
something has tried to kill me
and has failed.

## Related Resource

Mugshot of Martin Luther King Jr.

*Mugshot of Martin Luther King Jr., following his 1963 arrest in Birmingham, Alabama, 1963. Photograph, Birmingham Police Department.*

## Activities

1. **Warm-up**: Look closely at the photograph of Martin Luther King Jr. Write down all the words that might help someone imagine this image.
2. **Before Reading the Poem**: With a small group, discuss what you know about Martin Luther King Jr. Why do you think he looks the way he does in this photograph? Use details from the photograph to support your ideas.
3. **Reading the Poem**: Silently read "won't you celebrate with me" by Lucille Clifton. What do you notice about the poem? Note any

words, phrases, or poetic structures that stand out to you and any questions you might have.

4. **Listening to the Poem**: Enlist two volunteers and listen as the poem is read aloud twice. What did you hear that you did not previously notice when you were reading the poem? Write down any additional words and phrases that stand out to you.
5. **Small Group Discussion**: Gather in small groups and share what you noticed about the poem and how it is written. Why do you think Clifton does not use capital letters? How would you describe the type of language she uses? Why? Use evidence from the poem when making an interpretation.
6. **Large Group Discussion**: What do the photograph and the poem remind you of? Why is this important to remember today?
7. **Extension for Grades 7–8**: Clifton's sonnet invites the reader to "celebrate with me." What would you celebrate about your own life? Make a list, and write a poem or draw a picture of your own celebration.
8. **Extension for Grades 9–12**: Clifton uses language from several other poems, including "On Sitting Down to Read King Lear Once Again" by John Keats, "Song of Myself" by Walt Whitman, and Psalm 137 from the Bible. In small groups, research one of these passages and its author. From your research, identify what lines or images Clifton used. Share your findings with the whole group. How do these texts connect to Clifton's themes of self-made mythology and survival?

## More Context

### Historical Document

While in jail in Birmingham, King wrote a letter in response to some of his fellow clergymen, who had published a public letter criticizing his use of nonviolent direct action. He wrote,

> [Y]ou may well ask, why direct action? Why sit-ins, marches and so forth? Isn't negotiation a better path?' You are quite right in calling for negotiation. Indeed, this is the very purpose of direct action. Nonviolent direct action seeks to create such a crisis and foster such a tension that a community which has constantly refused to negotiate is forced to confront the issue.

Read more about the letter and the civil rights movement from the *Encyclopaedia Britannica*).

### Glossary Term

**Sonnet** a fourteen-line poem, traditionally written in iambic pentameter, that employs one of several rhyme schemes and adheres to a tightly structured thematic organization.

# The Pursuit of Equality

## "Black Laws"
### by Roger Reeves

Fuss, fight, and cutting the huckley-buck—Dear Malindy,
Underground, must I always return to the country of the dead,

To the coons catting about in the trees, the North Carolina pines
Chattering about sweetening bodies in their green whirring?

Do these letters predict my death—some sound of a twig
Breaking then a constant drowning—a butter bean drying

Beneath my nails? Casket, rascal, and corn bread cooling board.
Dear Malindy, when the muskrats fight in the swamp I knows

It's you causing my skull to rattle. You predicted my death
With my own baby teeth and a rancid moon beneath our legs.

No girl, my arm still here. The antlers on the mantle yet quiet.
All the ocean's water without me and yet in me. Never mind,

Malindy. They already shot the black boy on the road for dying
Without their permission. Yes, gal, I put on my nice suit. And wait.

## Related Resource

Black Lives Matter protest.

Tracy Meehleib, *Black Lives Matter Rally H Street, Washington, DC*, 2020. Photograph, Library of Congress.

## Activities

1. **Warm-up**: Write down one or two words that you associate with "early death." Share with a partner, then continue sharing with a small group.
2. **Before Reading the Poem**: Look closely at the image of a Black Lives Matter (BLM) rally from 2020. Write down all the words that would help someone imagine this photograph.

3. **Reading the Poem**: Silently read "Black Laws" by Roger Reeves. What do you notice about the poem? Note any words, phrases, or poetic structures that stand out to you and any questions you might have.
4. **Listening to the Poem**: Enlist two volunteers and listen as the poem is read aloud twice. What did you hear that you did not previously notice when you were reading the poem? Write down any additional words and phrases that stand out to you.
5. **Small Group Discussion**: Why is the speaker in the poem putting on his "nice suit?" What does he expect will happen to him? Support your thoughts with specific details and images from the poem.
6. **Large Group Discussion**: What kind of feeling is the speaker of the poem expressing? How might the events that led to the BLM movement relate to Reeves's poem? How are the poem's tone and the BLM movement's tone similar or different? How and why might both be important?
7. **Extension for Grades 7–8**: Write down words and phrases in the poem that rhyme or sound similar, and share with a partner. As a whole group, discuss what this kind of euphony brings to mind. Why would Reeves use this kind of language? Is the speaker of the poem talking to someone inside his community? How can you tell?
8. **Extension for Grades 9–12**: Read "Black Lives Matter: The Growth of a New Social Justice Movement" from Blackpast.org. In small groups, research one person or event important to the BLM movement, and share your findings with the whole group.

## More Context

### About This Poem by Roger Reeves

> 'Black Laws' is in conversation with so many things at once: Paul Laurence Dunbar and his dialect poems, the folk music group the Carolina Chocolate Drops, the deaths of Trayvon Martin and Jonathan Ferrell, lynching, John Berryman, elegy, and, most of all, the easily eradicable nature of black folks' lives in America. Every day I wonder if I'm next—the next Emmett Till, Trayvon Martin, or Jonathan Ferrell. I wonder who will sing for me when I'm gone.

## Glossary Term

**Euphony** a harmonious succession of words, pleasing to the ear.

## "Imagine"
*by Kamilah Aisha Moon*

> *after the news of the dead*
> *whether or not we knew them we are saying thank you*
> —W. S. Merwin

A blanket of fresh snow
makes any neighborhood idyllic.
Dearborn Heights indistinguishable from Baldwin Hills,
South Central even—
until a thawing happens and residents emerge
into the light. But it almost never snows in L.A.,
and snows often in this part of Michigan—
a declining wonderland, a place not to stand out
or be stranded like Renisha was.

Imagine a blonde daughter with a busted car
in a suburb where a brown homeowner
(not taking any chances)
blasts through a locked door first,
checks things out after—
around the clock coverage and the country beside itself
instead of the way it is now,
so quiet like a snowy night
and only the grief of a brown family (again)
around the Christmas tree, recalling
memories of Renisha playing
on the front porch, or catching flakes
as they fall and disappear
on her tongue.

They are left to imagine
what her life might have been.
We are left to imagine the day
it won't require imagination
to care about all of the others.

## Related Resource

Martin Luther King Jr. delivering his "I Have a Dream" speech.

Rowland Scherman, *Dr. Martin Luther King Jr. Speaking at the Civil Rights March on Washington, D.C.*, 1963. Photograph, National Archives.

## Activities

1. **Warm-up**: What is one wish you have for your home country? Share with a partner.
2. **Before Reading the Poem**: Listen to Martin Luther King Jr. deliver his "I Have a Dream" speech, beginning from 11:26, or page four if you are following along in the text. As you listen, follow along and circle the words and phrases that jump out at you. In small groups, discuss what you noticed in the speech. What was Dr. King's dream? Why do you think you noticed what you did?
3. **Reading the Poem**: Silently read "Imagine" by Kamilah Aisha Moon. What do you notice about the poem? Note any words, phrases, or poetic structures that stand out to you and any questions you might have.
4. **Listening to the Poem**: Enlist two volunteers and listen as the poem is read aloud twice. What did you hear that you did not previously notice when you were reading the poem? Write down any additional words and phrases that stand out to you.
5. **Small Group Discussion**: Speak with a partner about what you noticed from both readings. What is the speaker in the poem describing? How would you describe the tone? Use evidence from the poem to explain why you think so.
6. **Large Group Discussion**: In the second and third stanzas, there are two things the speaker asks the reader to imagine. What are they? How do these things relate to the dream that Dr. King describes? How do they relate to your wishes for your country?
7. **Extension for Grades 7–8**: Write a poem or prose piece that imagines a different ending to Renisha's story.

8. **Extension for Grades 9–12**: Why do you think Moon used the technique of asking readers to imagine different scenarios in this poem? How has imagination been involved in the circumstances of Renisha's death? Read "Renisha McBride Shooting: 'We May Never Know' Why" on NPR, and write a personal essay about how imagination can influence decision making, based on your life or relevant current events.

## More Context

### Article

Read more about Renisha McBride's life and the circumstances leading to her homicide from the *Say Their Names* project, an online memorial dedicated to sharing the stories of those whose lives have been lost to racial violence, hosted by Stanford's Green Library.

## Glossary Term

**Tone** a literary device that conveys the author's attitude toward the subject, speaker, or audience of a poem.

## "When Fannie Lou Hamer Said"
### by Mahogany L. Browne

*I'm sick and tired of being sick and tired*

    She meant

        No more turned cheek

        No more patience for the obstruction

        of black woman's right to vote

        & plant & feed her family

    She meant

        Equality will cost you your luxurious life

        If a Black woman can't vote

        If a brown baby can't be fed

        If we all don't have the same opportunity America promised

    She meant

        Ain't no mountain boulder enough

        to wan off a determined woman

    She meant

        Here

    Look at my hands

        Each palm holds a history

        of the 16 shots that chased me

        harm free from a plantation shack

    Look at my eyes

        Both these are windows

        these little lights of mine

    She meant

        Nothing but death can stop me

        from marching out a jail cell still a free woman

    She meant

        Nothing but death can stop me from running for Congress

She meant

> No black jack beating will stop my feet from working
>
> & my heart from swelling
>
> & my mouth from praying

She meant

> America! you will learn freedom feels like
>
> butter beans, potatoes & cotton seeds
>
> picked by my sturdy hands

She meant

Look

Victoria Gray, Anna Divine & Me

In our rightful seats on the house floor

She meant

> Until my children
>
> & my children's children
>
> & they babies too
>
> can March & vote
>
> & get back in interest
>
> what was planted
>
> in this blessed land

She meant

> I ain't stopping America
>
> I ain't stopping America

*Not even death* can take away from my woman's hands

what I've rightfully earned

## Related Resource

Fannie Lou Hamer poster.

Fannie Lou Hamer. *Elect Mrs. Fannie Lou Hamer, State Senator*, 1971. Broadside, Mississippi Department of Archives and History.

## Activities

1. **Warm-up**: Look carefully at Fannie Lou Hamer's election poster and the quote, "I'm sick and tired of being sick and tired." What do you notice?
2. **Before Reading the Poem**: Watch the PBS video exploring Fannie Lou Hamer's testimony. Why was Hamer's testimony so poignant? What connections can you make between her words and today?
3. **Reading the Poem**: Silently read "What Fannie Lou Hamer Said" by Mahogany L. Browne. What do you notice about the poem? Note any words, phrases, or poetic structures that stand out to you and any questions you might have.
4. **Listening to the Poem**: Enlist two volunteers and listen as the poem is read aloud twice. What did you hear that you did not previously notice when you were reading the poem? Write down any additional words and phrases that stand out to you.
5. **Small Group Discussion**: Share what you noticed in the poem with a small group of students. Based on the details you just shared, how might you describe Fannie Lou Hamer? What is she fighting for?
6. **Large Group Discussion**: In what ways is this poem a call to action and a celebration of Hamer's work? What is the significance of the epigraph in the poem?
7. **Extension for Grades 7–8**: Research the Voting Rights Act of 1965 and the current state of voter suppression. Individually or in a

small group, create an illustrated history of voting rights in the United States, and make sure to highlight activists and pioneers.
8. **Extension for Grades 9–12**: Research more about the Voting Rights Act of 1965 and the current state of voter suppression. Participate in a fishbowl discussion about what you learned and the current role of voting in U.S. politics.

## More Context

### Poems

In partnership with the New York Philharmonic, the Academy of American Poets commissioned nineteen women poets, including Mahogany L. Browne, to write poems marking the centennial of the passage of the Nineteenth Amendment. Read the poems.

## Glossary Term

**Epigraph** a quotation set at the beginning of a literary work or one of its divisions to suggest its theme.

## "The Cabbage Butterfly"
*by Minnie Bruce Pratt*

The human brain wants to complete—

The poem too easy? Bored. The poem too hard?
Angry. What's this one about? Around the block
the easy summer weather, the picture-puff clouds
adrift in the blue sky that's no paint-by-numbers.

In the corner garden, the cabbage butterfly
bothers the big leafy heads, trying to complete
its life cycle by hatching a horned monster to
chew holes in the green cloth manufactured so
laboriously by seed germ from air, water,
light, dirt. There's no end to this, yes, no end.

Even when we want to stop, stop, stop! Even
when someone else calls us *monster*. Even when
we fear and hope that we will not have the final
word.

**Related Resource**

Cabbage butterfly.

Joanna Gilkeson, *Cabbage White Butterfly*, 2020. Photo, U.S. Fish and Wildlife Service Pacific Southwest Region.

### Activities

1. **Warm-up**: Write down several words that describe how you feel when you can't complete something you really want to finish. Share your words with a partner.

2. **Before Reading the Poem**: Silently read information about the cabbageworm to yourself. Look carefully at the included photos and circle the words in the article that seem important, as well as the words that are unfamiliar to you. In groups of four, share what you learned about the cabbageworm and help each other define the words you don't know.
3. **Reading the Poem**: Silently read "The Cabbage Butterfly" by Minnie Bruce Pratt. What do you notice about the poem? Note any words, phrases, or poetic structures that stand out to you and any questions you might have.
4. **Listening to the Poem**: Listen to the audio of Minnie Bruce Pratt reading her poem twice. What did you hear that you did not previously notice when you were reading the poem? Write down any additional words and phrases that stand out to you.
5. **Small Group Discussion**: How does what you learned about the life cycle of the cabbageworm relate to the second stanza of the poem? What might have no end?
6. **Large Group Discussion**: Designate someone from each small group to report about what you thought was happening in the second stanza. Keeping the second stanza in mind, what might "we" in the twelfth line want to "stop, stop, stop!"? Why might someone else call them a "monster"? What might be "the final/word"?
7. **Extension for Grades 7–8**: How would you feel if someone thought you were a monster? What would you do about it? Discuss these questions with a partner, and write two paragraphs that answer them.
8. **Extension for Grades 9–12**: Why do you think Bruce Pratt wrote the first line? What was she trying to complete? Write a short essay that argues why you think this poem is complete or why not.

## More Context

### About This Poem by Minnie Bruce Pratt

> During the years that I wrote and revised this poem, my lover, and ultimately spouse, was gravely ill. Her medical care and my caregiving were deeply complicated by the anti-LGBTQ prejudices of some medical personnel, who certainly viewed us as 'monsters.' Every day for those years I took a walk to write a poem, trying to find a way to go on, a reason to even write poetry. The first draft of 'The Cabbage Butterfly' came from a walk I took on July 8, 2011. My beloved died in November 2014. I revised the poem four times before that loss and one time since. It is still not the final word.

## Glossary Term

**Line** a fundamental unit in verse that carries meaning horizontally across the page and vertically from one line to the next.

## "Things We Carry on the Sea"
*by Wang Ping*

We carry tears in our eyes: good-bye father, good-bye mother
We carry soil in small bags: may home never fade in our hearts
We carry names, stories, memories of our villages, our civilization
We carry scars from proxy wars of greed
We carry carnage of mining, droughts, floods, genocides
We carry dust of our families and neighbors incinerated in mushroom clouds
We carry our islands sinking under the sea
We carry our hands, feet, bones, hearts and best minds to start
a new life

We carry diplomas: medicine, engineer, nurse, education, math, poetry, even if they mean nothing to the other shore
We carry railroads, plantations, laundromats, bodegas, taco trucks, farms, factories, nursing homes, hospitals, schools, temples...
built on our ancestors' backs

We carry old homes along the spine, new dreams in our chests
We carry yesterday, today and tomorrow
We're orphans of the wars forced upon us
We're refugees of the sea drowning in plastic wastes
we came from the same mother in Africa
we're your children, sisters and brothers, father and mother

our tongues carry the same weight as we chant

爱(ai)，حب (hubb), ליבע (libe), amour, love
平安 (ping'an), سلام (salaam), shalom, paz, peace
希望 (xi'wang), أمل ('amal), hoffnung, esperanza, hope, hope, hope

As we drift ... from dream to dream ... sea to sea ...

# The Pursuit of Equality

## Related Resource

Vietnamese refugees in the South China Sea.

Kenneth Flemings, *South China Sea. Vietnamese refugees rest on the fantail of guided missile destroyer USS Towers (DDG 9) just after being rescued from their small boat*, 1981. Photograph, National Museum of the U.S. Navy.

## Activities

1. **Warm-up**: If you had to leave your home quickly because of a catastrophe, what are a few of the most important things you would take with you?
2. **Before Reading the Poem**: Silently read "Refugee Statistics" by the UN Refugee Agency. Take notes on the most important points in the article. With a partner, share the patterns you see among the conflicts from which people are fleeing.
3. **Reading the Poem**: Silently read "Things We Carry on the Sea" by Wang Ping. What do you notice about the poem? Note any words, phrases, or poetic structures that stand out to you and any questions you might have.
4. **Listening to the Poem**: Enlist two volunteers and listen as the poem is read aloud twice. What did you hear that you did not previously notice when you were reading the poem? Write down any additional words and phrases that stand out to you.
5. **Small Group Discussion**: Referring to what you noticed while reading and listening to the poem, discuss who you think is speaking in the poem. What details in the poem tell you this? What are they carrying with them? How do they carry these things?
6. **Large Group Discussion**: Why do you think Ping has chosen certain things for the people in the poem to carry? What do these things tell you about the people in the poem? What do the last five lines in the poem tell you? What did you learn from the poem that you did not learn from the article?

77

7. **Extension for Grades 7–10**: How do the things you listed in the warm-up relate to the things carried in this poem? Add five things to your list. Pick one and add three sensory details about the object.
8. **Extension for Grades 11–12**: What did you think or know about refugees before you read the article and this poem? What did you learn about refugees and immigration that you might not have known before? With a small group, conduct research about a current group of refugees and present your findings to your peers.

## More Context

### Lecture

In a lecture called "Tide of Voices: Why Poetry Matters Now," Mark Doty speaks about the importance of poetry during crisis. He says,

> The project of poetry, in a way, is to raise language to such a level that it can convey the precise nature of subjective experience. That the listener would envision not just a mouse but this particular one, in all its exact specificity, its perfect details. Such enchanted language could magically dissolve the barrier of skin and bone and separateness between us.

### Glossary Term

**List poem**   a deliberately organized poem containing a list of images or adjectives that build up to describe the poem's subject matter through an inventory of things.

# "Poem for the Poorest Country in the Western Hemisphere"

*by Danielle Legros Georges*

O poorest country, this is not your name.
You should be called beacon. You should

be called flame. Almond and bougainvillea,
garden and green mountain, villa and hut,

girl with red ribbons in her hair,
books under arm, charmed by the light

of morning, charcoal seller in black skirt,
encircled by dead trees. You, country,

are merchant woman and eager clerk,
grandfather at the gate, at the crossroads

with the flashlight, with all in sight.

## Related Resource

Family.

Danielle Legros Georges, *Family*, 2010. Photograph, Academy of American Poets.

## Activities

1. **Warm-up**: Say one word that represents what you know about Haiti. It is okay to say nothing, or pass.
2. **Before Reading the Poem**: Look closely at an image of a Haitian family and write down what you see. How would you describe this family to someone who has never seen this photo? What feelings are the family members expressing?

3. **Reading the Poem**: Silently read "Poem for the Poorest Country in the Western Hemisphere" by Danielle Legros Georges. What do you notice about the poem? Note any words, phrases, or poetic structures that stand out to you and any questions you might have.
4. **Listening to the Poem**: Enlist two volunteers and listen as the poem is read aloud twice. What did you hear that you did not previously notice when you were reading the poem? Write down any additional words and phrases that stand out to you.
5. **Small Group Discussion**: In a small group, share what you noticed in the poem and the photograph. Based on the details you just shared, how does the poem relate to the family photo?
6. **Large Group Discussion**: Does the imagery evoked by the poem communicate the same things as the imagery in the photograph? Why or why not? Use evidence from the poem and the photograph. Why might Georges want to share both this poem and a photo of a family?
7. **Extension for Grades 7–8**: Make a list of underrated things you love. Write a poem imitating the form: "You should not be called… You should be called." Use imagery and personification.
8. **Extension for Grades 9–12**: Read "Between midnight and eternity" by Haitian poet Kettly Mars, translated from the French by Nathan H. Dize. Both poems deal with place, family, and nature. Compare and contrast how Georges and Mars use poetic techniques to establish tone.

## More Context

### Article

In her article "Haitian Revolution (1791–1804)," Claudia Sutherland writes,

> The Haitian Revolution has often been described as the largest and most successful slave rebellion in the Western Hemisphere. Enslaved people initiated the rebellion in 1791 and by 1803 they had succeeded in ending not just slavery but French control over the colony. The Haitian Revolution, however, was much more complex, consisting of several revolutions going on simultaneously. These revolutions were influenced by the French Revolution of 1789, which would come to represent a new concept of human rights, universal citizenship, and participation in government.

Read more about the revolution and what has happened politically in Haiti since then.

### Glossary Term

**Personification** the attribution of human qualities to animals, inanimate objects, or abstract ideas.

## "A New National Anthem"
*by Ada Limón*

The truth is, I've never cared for the National
Anthem. If you think about it, it's not a good
song. Too high for most of us with "the rockets'
red glare" and then there are the bombs.
(Always, always there is war and bombs.)
Once, I sang it at homecoming and threw
even the tenacious high school band off key.
But the song didn't mean anything, just a call
to the field, something to get through before
the pummeling of youth. And what of the stanzas
we never sing, the third that mentions "no refuge
could save the hireling and the slave"? Perhaps
the truth is that every song of this country
has an unsung third stanza, something brutal
snaking underneath us as we absent-mindedly sing
the high notes with a beer sloshing in the stands
hoping our team wins. Don't get me wrong, I do
like the flag, how it undulates in the wind
like water, elemental, and best when it's humbled,
brought to its knees, clung to by someone who
has lost everything, when it's not a weapon,
when it flickers, when it folds up so perfectly
you can keep it until it's needed, until you can
love it again, until the song in your mouth feels
like sustenance, a song where the notes are sung
by even the ageless woods, the shortgrass plains,
the Red River Gorge, the fistful of land left
unpoisoned, that song that's our birthright,
that's sung in silence when it's too hard to go on,
that sounds like someone's rough fingers weaving
into another's, that sounds like a match being lit
in an endless cave, the song that says my bones
are your bones, and your bones are my bones,
and isn't that enough?

## Related Resource

Original manuscript of the "Star Spangled Banner."

Harris & Ewing, *Key, Francis Scott. Original Manuscript of "Star Spangled Banner,"* 1914. Photograph, Library of Congress.

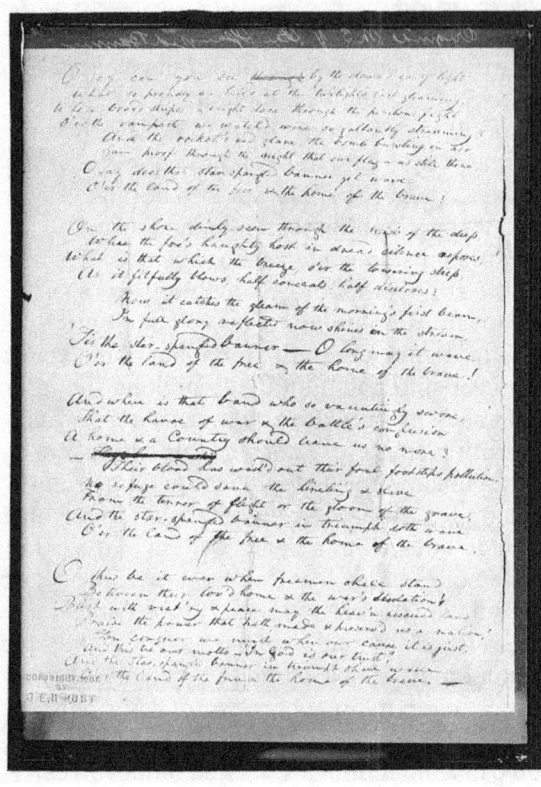

## Activities

1. **Warm-up**: Look at the image of Francis Scott Key's original manuscript of the "Star Spangled Banner." What stands out to you about the image?
2. **Before Reading the Poem**: Watch Whitney Houston sing the national anthem. What do you notice about her version? What did you like the most about it?
3. **Reading the Poem**: Silently read "A New National Anthem" by Ada Limón. What do you notice about the poem? Note any words, phrases, or poetic structures that stand out to you and any questions you might have.
4. **Listening to the Poem**: Enlist two volunteers and listen as the poem is read aloud twice. What did you hear that you did not previously notice when you were reading the poem? Write down any additional words and phrases that stand out to you.
5. **Small Group Discussion**: Share what you noticed in the poem with a small group. Based on the details you just shared, how are this poem and Houston's rendition both new versions of the national anthem?

6. **Large Group Discussion**: Read the entire text of the national anthem and respond in writing to this quote from the poem: "And what of the stanzas/we never sing, the third that mentions 'no refuge/could save the hireling and the slave'? Perhaps/the truth is that every song of this country/has an unsung third stanza, something brutal/snaking underneath us as we blindly sing…." Share your writing and thoughts with your peers. What is the brutal thing lurking underneath Key's national anthem? What does the speaker in the poem call for? Why?
7. **Extension for Grades 7–8**: Create your own version of an anthem, write a response to Limón's poem, or revise the national anthem.
8. **Extension for Grades 9–12**: Read Nikole Hannah-Jones's essay "The Idea of America." After reading Limón's poem and Hannah-Jones's essay, draft a poem, personal essay, or photo essay about your idea of America. What was the hardest part about drafting this idea?

## More Context

### Lecture

"Is 'make it new' essentially the enduring motto of America?" In his 2020 Blaney Lecture, Terrance Hayes asks readers and listeners to consider the history of American poetry, who we think of as important, and why.

## Glossary Term

**Revision** both a noun and a verb, revision can refer to the act of making a new, amended, improved, or up-to-date version of a text, or to that version itself.

### "Miss Mary Mack Introduces Her Wings"
*by Tyree Daye*

My name is   Miss Mary   Mack     Mack     Mack

    you sing it     my name

I turned into a bluebird last summer, I flew

through all the South. My wings are blue

and I touch the sky.

At first, I decided I was never coming back.

I took off my black

        housedress. I knew freedom

was not the act of flying,

    but the steady beat of wings.

It was my steady black,

    blue and my blues were gone,

I wanted to be

    a bird and became.

**Related Resource**

Bluebird.

Tom Koerner, *Mountain Bluebirds in Snow at Seedskadee National Wildlife Refuge*, 2020. Photograph, U.S. Fish and Wildlife Service Mountain Prairie Region.

## Activities

1. **Warm-up**: Play a clapping game with a partner (for example, "Patty-Cake," "Miss Mary Mack," "Down by the Banks"). If you don't know any, research one as a group and learn how to play it. How does playing this game make you feel? Why?
2. **Before Reading the Poem**: Look at this image of a bluebird. What do you notice about the bird?
3. **Reading the Poem**: Silently read "Miss Mary Mack Introduces Her Wings" by Tyree Daye. What do you notice about the poem? Note any words, phrases, or poetic structures that stand out to you and any questions you might have.

4. **Listening to the Poem**: Watch Daye read his poem twice. What did you hear that you did not previously notice when you were reading the poem? Write down any additional words and phrases that stand out to you.
5. **Small Group Discussion**: Share what you noticed about the poem with a small group of students. Based on the poem, the warm-up game, and the photograph of the bluebird, how does "Miss Mary Mack [introduce] Her Wings?" What do you think of the lines: "I knew freedom/was not the act of flying, but the steady beat of wings"?
6. **Large Group Discussion**: What do you notice about the poem's structure and its use of repetition? What does this make you think of? How does it impact your reading of the poem? How would you describe Miss Mary Mack?
7. **Extension for Grades 7–8**: Write a poem or create a visual illustration based on the poem or selected lines from it.
8. **Extension for Grades 9–12**: Conduct research about common childhood games in a country you are unfamiliar with. How do this country's childhood games compare to your childhood games? Share your findings with a group.

## More Context

### Article

Watch clips of clapping games in "Around the World in 5 Kids Games," an interactive feature story from *The New York Times*, which features videos of students playing clapping games in Arabic, Haitian Creole, Korean, Polish, and Spanish, as well as interviews with the students and educators.

## Glossary Term

**Repetition**  the poetic technique of repeating the same word or phrase multiple times within a poem or work.

## "I Want the Wide American Earth"
*by Carlos Bulosan*

Before the brave, before the proud builders and workers,
I say I want the wide American earth,
Its beautiful rivers and long valleys and fertile plains,
Its numberless hamlets and expanding towns and towering cities,
Its limitless frontiers, its probing intelligence,
For all the free.
                      Free men everywhere in my land—
This wide American earth—do not wander homeless,
And are not alone; friendship is our bread, love our air;
And we call each other comrade, each growing with the other,
Each a neighbor to the other, boundless in freedom.

I say I want the wide American earth....
I say to you defenders of freedom, builders of peace,
I say to you democratic brothers, comrades of love:
Their judges lynch us, their police hunt us;
Their armies and navies and airmen terrorize us;
Their thugs and stoolies and murderers kill us;
They take away bread from our children;
They ravage our women;
They deny life to our elders.
                    But I say we have the truth
On our side, we have the future with us;
We are millions everywhere,
on seas and oceans and lands;
In air;
On water and all over this very earth.
We are millions working together.
We are building, creating, molding life.
We are shaping the shining structures of love.
We are everywhere, we are everywhere.
We are there when they sentence us to prison for telling the truth;
We are there when they conscript us to fight their wars;
We are there when they throw us in concentration camps;
We are there when they come at dawn with their guns.
We are there, we are there,
and we say to them:

"You cannot frighten us with your bombs and deaths;
You cannot drive us away from our land with your hate and disease;
You cannot starve us with your war programs and high prices;
You cannot command us with your nothing,
Because you are nothing but nothing;
You cannot put us all in your padded jails;
You cannot snatch the dawn of life from us!"

And we say to them:

"Remember, remember,
We shall no longer wear rags, eat stale bread, live in darkness;
We shall no longer kneel on our knees to your false gods;
We shall no longer beg you for a share of life.
Remember, remember,
O remember in the deepest midnight of your fear,
We shall emulate the wonder of our women,
The ringing laughter of our children,
The strength and manhood of our men
With a true and honest and powerful love!"

And we say to them:

"We are the creators of a flowering race!"

I say I want the wide American earth.
I say to you too, sharer of my delights and thoughts,
I say this deathless truth,
And more—
    For look, watch, listen:
With a stroke of my hand I open the dawn of a new world,
Lift up the beautiful horizon of a new life;
All for you, comrade and my love.
    See:
The magnificent towers of our future is afire with truth,
And growing with the fuel of the heart of my heart,
and unfolding and unfolding, and flowering and flowering
In the bright new sun of our world;
All for you, comrade and my wife.
    And see:
I cry, I weep with joy,
And my tears are the tears of my people....

Before the brave, before the proud builders and workers,
I say I want the wide American earth
For all the free,
I want the wide American earth for my people,
I want my beautiful land.
I want it with my rippling strength and tenderness
Of love and light and truth
For all the free—

## Related Resource

Woody Guthrie.

Al Aumuller/ New York World–Telegram and the Sun Newspaper, *Woody Guthrie, half-length portrait, seated, facing front, playing a guitar that has a sticker attached reading: This Machine Kills Fascists*, 1943. Photograph, Library of Congress.

## Activities

1. **Warm-up**: Listen to the song "This Land Is Your Land" by Woody Guthrie and look up the lyrics if needed. What words or phrases stand out to you in the song? Why? What message do you gather from the song? Why?
2. **Before Reading the Poem**: Look closely at the comic "Building America" by Ming Doyle. What do you notice? What stands out to you? Why?
3. **Reading the Poem**: Silently read "I Want the Wide American Earth" by Carlos Bulosan. What do you notice about the poem? Note any words, phrases, or poetic structures that stand out to you and any questions you might have.
4. **Listening to the Poem**: Enlist two volunteers and listen as the poem is read aloud twice. What did you hear that you did not previously notice when you were reading the poem? Write down any additional words and phrases that stand out to you.
5. **Small Group Discussion**: Share what you noticed about the poem with a small group. Based on the details you just shared, the song, and the comic, what do you notice about the poem? What do you make of the title "I Want the Wide American Earth?" Is America wide? How or why?
6. **Whole Group Discussion**: What story does the poem tell about America? How does this compare to or contrast with your own story of America? Who or what has shaped America? How does anaphora impact your reading of the poem? How is this important to the poem? Why? What themes are most present in the poem?

7. **Extension for Grades 7–8**: Think back to the comic you read. Draw your own comic that tells your own story of America, or a place that is important to you.
8. **Extension for Grades 9–12**: Research Woody Guthrie, the history, and the labor movement surrounding "This Land Is Your Land." Using what you've learned, write a response drawing comparisons to Guthrie and Bulosan's work. What does their work have in common?

## More Context

### Exhibit

Learn more about Carlos Bulosan, who in addition to being a poet, was an influential Filipino American author and activist from the "Author, Poet, and Worker: The World of Carlos Bulosan" exhibit by the University of Washington Libraries.

## Glossary Term

**Anaphora**  a poetic technique in which successive phrases or lines begin with the same words, often resembling a litany.

## "A House Called Tomorrow"
*by Alberto Ríos*

You are not fifteen, or twelve, or seventeen—
You are a hundred wild centuries

And fifteen, bringing with you
In every breath and in every step

Everyone who has come before you,
All the yous that you have been,

The mothers of your mother,
The fathers of your father.

If someone in your family tree was trouble,
A hundred were not:

The bad do not win—not finally,
No matter how loud they are.

We simply would not be here
If that were so.

You are made, fundamentally, from the good.
With this knowledge, you never march alone.

You are the breaking news of the century.
You are the good who has come forward

Through it all, even if so many days
Feel otherwise. But think:

When you as a child learned to speak,
It's not that you didn't know words—

It's that, from the centuries, you knew so many,
And it's hard to choose the words that will be your own.

From those centuries we human beings bring with us
The simple solutions and songs,

The river bridges and star charts and song harmonies
All in service to a simple idea:

That we can make a house called tomorrow.
What we bring, finally, into the new day, every day,

Is ourselves. And that's all we need
To start. That's everything we require to keep going.

Look back only for as long as you must,
Then go forward into the history you will make.

The Pursuit of Equality

Be good, then better. Write books. Cure disease.
Make us proud. Make yourself proud.

And those who came before you? When you hear thunder,
Hear it as their applause.

## Related Resource

Family tree.

Chapman Brothers Lithography Chicago, *Family Record of [Blank]*, 1888. Lithograph, Library of Congress.

## Activities

1. **Warm-up**: Ask your parents, guardians, or family members to tell you what they know about their ancestors. Write down what they tell you using the family tree from 1888 as a model.
2. **Before Reading the Poem**: Tell your partner about the history of your family or other respected elders. What did you learn? Did you discover any surprises? What else do you wish you knew?
3. **Reading the Poem**: Silently read "A House Called Tomorrow" by Alberto Ríos. What do you notice about the poem? Note any words, phrases, or poetic structures that stand out to you and any questions you might have.
4. **Listening to the Poem**: Enlist two volunteers and listen as the poem is read aloud twice. What did you hear that you did not previously notice when you were reading the poem? Write down any additional words and phrases that stand out to you.

5. **Small Group Discussion**: What does the speaker in the poem say about past generations? How does the speaker think these generations address the reader? Why do you think Ríos chose to write the poem in couplets? Cite evidence from the poem.
6. **Large Group Discussion**: What do you think the speaker of the poem means when they say "we can make a house called tomorrow"? With what should we build this house? How should we build it?
7. **Extension for Grades 7–10**: How will you build a "house called tomorrow" based on what you have learned from your ancestors? Share what you will do to build this house, and create an anthology with everyone's response.
8. **Extension for Grades 11–12**: How will you contribute to building "a house called tomorrow" that is more equitable for this country's residents and less divided? How will you rely on values transmitted by your ancestors as you contribute to a positive future? Create and display a collage of images that answers these questions.

## More Context

### Poem

In "Some Thoughts on the Integrity of the Single Line in Poetry," Alberto Ríos writes in praise of

> lines that are long in their moment, that make me linger and give me the effect of having encountered something, something worth stopping for—the antithesis of our times, which seem to be all about getting somewhere else, and fast, and we're late already.

### Glossary Term

**Second-person point of view** the speaker of a poem tells a story about "you" or describes a series of events, actions, and scenes that include "you."

# 3 Afterword by Major Jackson

Poetry is a magical place where one is likely to discover oneself, what one imagines, hears, believes, and dreams. But more compellingly, we are likely to discover other human beings: their rituals and customs, their sympathies and affections, even how they talk. In a democracy such as ours, made up of people from all walks of life and backgrounds, hearing the richness of our nation in artful speech proves indispensable in cultivating compassion and understanding for those outside our life experiences. While not its only function, poetry also thrives beyond the affairs of humankind; poetry deepens our appreciation for the wealth of experiences and perspectives in our neighborhoods, schools, grocery stores, public transportation, and communities.

For nearly three decades, I have taught in university classrooms, writers' conferences, and high schools throughout the United States. I never cease to marvel at the harmonious spirit of affirmation that poetry engenders among people of radically different backgrounds and ages. The reading and writing of poetry creates opportunities to map our interior thoughts and feelings. And how confident and devoted we become when we claim our narratives and voice our realities. And how less fearful and alone we are when we hear another person give testimony to their life. We discover we are more alike than we are different. Poetry written in a pluralistic society enhances our regard for each other while simultaneously honoring the sound and texture of the lone human voice speaking to the vastness of our collectivity.

Walt Whitman famously wrote, "[I hear] [e]ach singing what belongs to him or her and to none else/[...] with open mouths their strong melodious songs." Harlem Renaissance poet Langston Hughes also listened to America and heard the country's marginalized citizens, its immigrants and poor alike, and wrote, "Let it be the dream it used to be [...] O, let America be America again."

To teach poetry is to attune students to the spirit of a country aiming to make real its precious ideals of freedom and equality. We celebrate the inclusive nature of America but also attempt to rectify our history of colonialism, subjugation, and injustices. From Phyllis Wheatley's early colonial poems to Ada Limón's poems about family and the body, our poetry documents our history and struggles as a nation but also points to a place in our literature where we can heal. Joy Harjo's poem "Perhaps the World Ends Here" offers a salient metaphor of a kitchen table to understand the communal agency of poetry: "At this table we sing with joy, with sorrow. We pray of suffering and remorse. /We give thanks." American poetry is a literary record of treasured voices gathered who become emblematic of us all.

*Teach This Poem, Volume 2: Equality for All* underscores one of the main tenets of my own teaching—that is, cultivating a radiant attentiveness within students. When we teach poems, we provide a foundation of reading, writing, and interpretative skills that serve students well into their futures. But we also instruct them to take stock and measure the world around them through poetry's powers of evocation. We urge them to see life as sacred and language as a force that shapes their realities. My lesson plans are full of poems about animals, trees, forests, and bodies of water.

*Teach This Poem, Volume 2: Equality for All* widens the canvas—it includes poems and exercises that encourage students to become witnesses to the larger story that is America. Here are poems that urge us to remember forgotten histories and figures, to treasure the land, to revel in our cultural diversity, to dream of a world we wish to live in. In Whitmanian fashion, Filipino American poet Carlos Bulosan proclaims, "I want the wide American earth/For all the free." In this way, students are invited to go beyond the novelistic sense of their own selves and anchor themselves in a sea of consciousness that foregrounds our collective humanity.

Occasionally, poetry is called into a greater service that feels spiritual. The poets' words live in us as an antidote to the grand mysteries and emerge ultimately for the greater good of the communities we belong to and those we cannot imagine. Even the most personal poems tend to reach wide and divine our presence on Earth as they aim for clarity and not obfuscation, candor in lieu of the willfully enigmatic and private. Some poems reach so far into the future that their truths become etched in our beings; they sing long into our ears.

Reading *Teach This Poem: Volume 2, Equality for All*, I am reminded that despite advances in artificial intelligence, the human brain is still the fastest computer on Earth. From my experience, teaching poetry opens pathways to complex thinking. Through encounters with poetry's use of metaphor, imagery, rhythmic language, form, and syntax, students expand their capacity for apprehending complex thoughts. Most importantly, exposing students to poems that think through real world problems encourages them to develop an emotional response to issues that impact them.

Poetry does not have to exist in some lofty fervor of the learned. When we teach students to read and write poetry, we endow them with a capacity to articulate their unique worldview, to express themselves without constraints, to locate language that most reveals their understanding and epiphanies. For a moment, the poem temporarily satiates their curiosities, but it then moves on to forward them into more questions.

The poems in *Teach This Poem, Volume 2: Equality for All* are more than literary artifacts; they represent the highest forms of human speech. They show us how we dream in language that is free of distortions, that normalizes thinking big about existence, that puts forth the imagination as a way of living in the world.

# 4 Glossary of Poetic Terms

**Alliteration** the repetition of consonant sounds, particularly at the beginning of words.

Alliteration describes multiple words grouped together that contain the same first consonant sound. Alliteration is used in common speech and all forms of literature, but it is especially prominent in poetry, which places emphasis on sound and the sound of words. A well-known example of alliteration is William Shakespeare's "Sonnet 30: When to the sessions of sweet silent thought." The words "sessions," "sweet," "silent," "summon," "sigh," and "sought" all begin with the same consonant sound and occur close together in the first three lines of the poem.

See also consonance.

**Allusion** a reference to a person, event, or literary work.

Allusions are implied or indirect, and poems with allusions do not necessarily cite the work or historical event they are referencing. When poets use allusions, they are assuming a shared knowledge between themselves and the reader. Traditional Western literature often makes allusions to other works in literature, the Bible, and Greek mythology with the understanding that most readers will have experience with the texts. However, some poets intentionally use obscure allusions in their writing, knowing that few readers will understand the references. Allusions can be used to enhance a text by bringing in context or background knowledge.

**Anaphora** a poetic technique in which successive phrases or lines begin with the same words, often resembling a litany.

The term "anaphora" comes from the Greek for "a carrying up or back." As one of the oldest-known literary devices, anaphora is used in much of the world's religious and devotional poetry, including numerous biblical hymns in the *Book of Psalms*. The repetition of anaphora can be as simple as a single word or as long as an entire phrase. Anaphora can create a driving rhythm by the recurrence of the same sound, and it can also intensify the emotion of the poem.

See also repetition.

**Anthropomorphism** the attribution of human form, traits, actions, or emotions to an animal, object, or nonhuman being.

The term "anthropomorphism" derives from the Greek word *anthrōpomorphos* meaning "having human form or qualities." Distinct from personification, anthropomorphism does not rely on figurative language to provide human attributes in a metaphorical or representative way. Instead, anthropomorphism is used to display human traits and attributes of human behavior in animals, objects, nonhuman, or supernatural beings incapable of having such characteristics. For example, Homer uses anthropomorphism in his epic poems *The Odyssey* and *The Iliad* by assigning human qualities and tendencies to Greek gods, including Aphrodite and Ares.

**Ars poetica** a poem that explores the art of poetry by examining the role of the poet and their relationship to the poem and the act of writing.

Among the first known treatises on poetry, Horace's "Ars Poetica," also referred to as "Epistle to the Pisos," is literally translated as "The Art of Poetry" or "On the Art of Poetry." Composed some time between 20 BC and 13 BC, the poem outlines principles of poetry, including knowledge, decorum, and sincerity, and introduced Horace as both a poet and critic. First translated into English by Ben Jonson and published in 1640, the treatise set standards for poetry and criticism and laid the foundation for an entire category of poetic work still being written today. While the focus of ars poetica has shifted from didactic argument toward more introspective takes on a poet's individual art, Horace's treatise continues to serve as the model for poets to examine their writing process and relationship to poetry.

**Ballad** a plot-driven song with one or more characters, often constructed in quatrain stanzas.

A ballad tends to show rather than tell the reader what's happening, describing each crucial moment in the trail of events as the poem leads to a dramatic conclusion. To convey a sense of emotional urgency, a ballad is often constructed in quatrain stanzas, each line containing as few as three or four stresses and either the second and fourth lines or all alternating lines rhyming. During the Renaissance, creating and selling ballad broadsides became a popular practice, and ballads began to make their way into print in fifteenth-century England from European folk tradition. The ballad has been used by acclaimed poets of various poetic movements from Romantic poet Emily Dickinson to Modernist poet Ezra Pound and beyond.

**Caesura** a pause for a beat in the rhythm of a verse, often indicated by a line break or by punctuation.

The term "caesura" comes from the Latin past participle stem of *caedere*, meaning "to cut down." There are three types of caesura: initial, medial, and terminal. Initial caesura is when the pause appears at or near the beginning of a line; medial caesura occurs in the middle of the line; terminal caesura is when the pause appears at the end or near the end of a line. Historically, medial caesura was primarily used in many classical meters. Today, modern poetic forms and contemporary poets are flexible with the use of caesura.

See also meter.

**Cento** a form also known as a collage poem and composed entirely of lines from poems by other poets.

From the Latin word for "patchwork," the cento (or collage poem) is a poetic form composed entirely of lines from poems by other poets. Modern centos are often witty, creating irony or humor from the juxtaposition of images and ideas, although they have also increasingly been used as love poems or to interrogate the historical record.

**Concrete poetry** poetry that creates physical shapes with language; a concrete poem is as much a piece of visual art made with words as it is a work of poetry.

European artists Max Bill and Öyving Fahlström originated the term "concrete poetry" in the early 1950s. During this period, concrete poems were intended to be abstract and without allusion to a recognizable shape, like the E. E. Cummings poem "r-p-o-p-h-e-s-s-a-g-r," which uses spacing and punctuation to create a distinct form on the page but doesn't evoke any associations to an identifiable object. The movement spread, reached its height of popularity in the 1960s, and became less abstract. Poets began to adopt concrete poetry as a specific poetic form that used words, often the repetition of the same word, to depict a recognizable object, shape, or pattern.

Contemporary concrete poetry has evolved to include photography, film, and even soundscapes.

**Consonance** the repetition of similar consonant sounds.

Consonance describes multiple words grouped together that contain the same consonant sound. Unlike alliteration, which refers to the use of the same *initial* consonant sound, consonance refers to when the sound is used anywhere in the words within the grouping and may create a subtler effect. Like all sound techniques, it is used in common speech and all forms of literature, but it is especially prominent in poetry, which places emphasis on sound and the sound of words.

See also alliteration.

**Contrapuntal** a poetic form that interweaves two or more poems to create a single poem that can be read in multiple ways depending on how the poem is designed on the page.

Contrapuntal comes from the Italian word *contrapunto*, which means "pertaining to counterpoint" and "backstitch." The poetic form is inspired by contrapuntal, or counterpoint, music, which is defined as the use of multiple independent melodies playing simultaneously with an equal weight where no melody dominates. Russian novelist and symbolist poet Andrei Bely is noted for employing the contrapuntal form and devices of music in his long poem "Pervoe Svidanie." Contrapuntal as a poetic form reemerged in the twenty-first century with poets such as Brian Bilston, Sarah Cooper, Tarfia Faizullah, and Tyehimba Jess. The theme of a contrapuntal poem varies, and there are no structural constraints of meter or rhyme. The key feature of contrapuntal poetry is how the poem appears on the page, thus sharing similar visual characteristics with concrete or shape poetry, as well as postmodern aesthetics.

**Couplet** a two-line stanza, or two successive lines of verse, rhymed or unrhymed.

In French, *couplet* is the diminutive of couple. In poetry, the two lines in a couplet can rhyme with one another and have the same meter, or not. Not all couplets have similar syllabic patterns. A couplet can be part of a poem or be a poem on its own. A well-known type of couplet in English poetry is the heroic couplet, which is written in rhymed iambic pentameter. A couplet can be either open or closed. If open, a couplet is a run-on couplet, meaning the first line flows to the second as a continuous sentence. If closed, the couplet is a formal couplet featuring two separate sentences.

See also line, meter, and stanza.

**Ekphrasis** the use of vivid language to describe or respond to a work of visual art.

Borrowed from the Greek term *ékphrasis*, or "description," early ekphrasis was used as a vivid description of a thing. The purpose of ekphrasis was to describe a thing with such detail that the reader could envision it as if it were present. Ekphrastic writing became important in the second half of the eighteenth century when a public demand for descriptions of art arose. There were no accurate reproductions of works of visual art to distribute to the public, so the art had to be shared through language. The goal for these ekphrastic writers was to impart a visual experience on their readers.

In the nineteenth and twentieth centuries, ekphrasis continued to change, exchanging the tradition of elaborate description for interpretation or interrogation. The poet John Hollander wrote that poets' new ways of writing about art included "addressing the image, making it speak, speaking of it interpretively, meditating upon the moment of viewing it, and so forth."

**Enjambment** the continuation of a sentence or clause across a poetic line break.

Enjambment comes from the French word *enjamber*, which means "to stride over." Enjambment was first formally used in the mid-nineteenth century, but the poetic device can be traced back to biblical verses and the works of Homer. An enjambed line is the opposite of an end-stopped line, in that the running-over of a sentence or phrase across one poetic line to the next is done without punctuation, whereas an end-stopped line ends a poetic line with punctuation. Enjambed lines minimize the difference of sound between verse and prose, while increasing the speed and pacing of a poem. By the twentieth century, enjambment became a key feature in poetry.

**End-stopped line** a metrical line that contains a complete phrase or sentence, or a poetic line that ends with punctuation.

End-stopped lines are the opposite of enjambed lines in that end-stopped lines contain complete thoughts, phrases, or sentences. These lines give the reader moments to pause at a line break. Usually, one can tell a poetic line is end-stopped by looking to see if there is punctuation at the end. The punctuation could be internal (e.g., comma, semicolon, colon, em dash) or external (e.g., period, exclamation mark, question mark). Many poets interweave end-stopped and enjambed lines in their poetry, whereas others will compose poems entirely of end-stopped lines.

**Epigraph** a quotation set at the beginning of a literary work or one of its divisions to suggest its theme.

Epigraphs first became popular in Europe during the early eighteenth century, accompanying the rise of a literate middle class. Before this time, to be literate meant one was familiar with the classical tradition. If a person could read English, they were presumably well-versed in the work of writers like Ovid, Homer, and Virgil. Authors did not need to tie themselves to previous works with an epigraph because readers were assumed to make connections themselves. Epigraphs are used not just to make connections between works but also to set the tone for a poem, to present text to which the poem will then respond, or to introduce the reader to the topic addressed.

**Epistolary poem** a poem of direct address that reads as a letter, also known as an epistle.

Epistle derives from the Latin word *epistula* meaning letter. Epistolary poems are quite literally poems that read as letters. As poems of direct address, they can be intimate and colloquial or formal and measured. The subject matter can range from philosophical investigation to a declaration of love or a list of errands. Epistles can take any form, from heroic couplets to free verse.

**Erasure** a form of found poetry wherein a poet takes an existing text and erases, blacks out, or otherwise obscures a large portion of the text, creating a wholly new work from what remains.

Erasure poetry, also known as blackout poetry, is a form of found poetry wherein a poet takes an existing text and erases, blacks out, or otherwise obscures a large portion of the text, creating a wholly new work from what remains. Erasure poetry may be used as a means of collaboration, creating a new text from an old one and thereby starting a dialogue between the two, or as a means of confrontation, a challenge to a preexisting text.

**Euphony** a harmonious succession of words, pleasing to the ear.

Euphony comes to English from the Greek *euphonos*, meaning "musical" or "sweet-voiced." A building block of poetry, euphony is created through the manipulation of sound, including rhythm, meter, assonance, consonance, alliteration, or the breaking of those patterns. The same techniques can be used to create the opposite effect: *cacophony*, or musical dissonance.

See also alliteration, caesura, consonance, meter, repetition, and rhyme.

**Form** the structure of a poem, including its line lengths, line breaks, meter, stanza lengths, and rhyme schemes.

Every poem has a form, but some forms are unique to individual poems and some are more widely used and include their own set of rules and parameters. Specific poetic forms include sonnet, villanelle, haiku, and prose poem. Form refers to the appearance and sound of the poem, but it can also influence the tone or purpose of the poem. For example, many sonnets are love poems, so the tone of a poem written in the sonnet form might be reverent or yearning. Although some forms observe specific rules, poets often break these rules to subvert readers' expectations so the deviation from a particular form becomes an essential aspect of the poem.

**Free verse** poetry that isn't dictated by an established form or meter, often influenced by the rhythms of speech.

Free verse describes poetry that does not follow a set metrical system or rhyme scheme. A rhythmic pattern of sound emerges in free-verse lines, yet there is no metrical plan in the composition used by the poet. Enjambment is often used in free-verse poetry, which often reflects the natural rhythms of speech. Poets from Walt Whitman to William Carlos Williams popularized the style in contemporary poetry. The opposite of free verse is formal verse, which adheres to a strict metric and rhyme system. Blank verse is poetry with a strict meter, but with no rhyme scheme.

See also form and meter.

**Haiku** a poem traditionally composed of three lines with seventeen syllables, written in a 5/7/5 syllable count in English, and often focused on images from nature.

Haiku began in thirteenth-century Japan as the opening phrase of renga, an oral poem that was generally a hundred stanzas long and composed syllabically. The much shorter haiku broke away from renga in the sixteenth century and was mastered a century later by the poet Matsuo Basho. As the form evolved, many of its traditional traits—including its famous syllabic pattern—have been routinely broken. However, the philosophy of haiku has been preserved: the focus on a brief moment in time, the use of provocative and colorful images, an ability to be read in one breath, and a sense of sudden enlightenment.

**Idiom** a short expression peculiar to a language, people, or place that conveys a figurative meaning without a literal interpretation of the words used in the phrase.

From the late Latin *idioma*, which means "a peculiarity in language," idioms have been used for centuries. In French, *idiome* means a "form of speech peculiar to a people or place," and by the 1620s, idiom also meant a "phrase or expression peculiar to a language." Idioms are set phrases, in that they only make sense if they are used exactly, such as a dime a dozen, piece of cake, and passed away. Writers will use idioms to intensify an image, express an idea, or approximate everyday speech. William Shakespeare used idioms as a literary device in multiple works, including in Othello, Act III, Scene III "[O, beware, my lord, of jealousy]," where jealousy is personified as the green-eyed monster.

**Imagery** language in a poem that represents a sensory experience.

Imagery uses vivid and figurative language to engage the senses and depict an object, person, scene, or feeling. The five types of imagery—visual, auditory, olfactory, tactile, and gustatory—relate to the five senses. Writers use imagery to build a specific sensory experience for readers to imagine and relate to. Literary devices such as simile and metaphor can be used to create imagery.

**Line** a fundamental unit in verse that carries meaning horizontally across the page and vertically from one line to the next.

A line in poetry is a group of words, most commonly arranged horizontally, that can vary in length and can adhere to a strict meter, or not. Lines determine a poem's syntax, tone, and rhythm. Understanding a line is a major element of understanding poetry, because a line's length and position relative to other lines help carry the meaning and music of a poem. A line that has a strict meter is called a verse, or a metrical line of poetic composition.

See also meter.

**List poem** a deliberately organized poem containing a list of images or adjectives that build up to describe the poem's subject matter through an inventory of things.

List poetry, also known as catalog verse, is a poetic form and literary device that highlights an intentional catalog of people, places, things, and ideas in relation to each other, evoking an emotion or story. Its roots date back to roughly 100 AD when parts of the Bible were written. Verses of lists are also found in Homer's *Iliad*, which dates back to the early eighth or late seventh century BC. A list poem has no specific rhyme scheme or meter and often features repetition, in particular anaphora. Famous examples include Walt Whitman's "I Hear America Singing" and "Song of Myself."

**Lyric poetry** non-narrative poetry that expresses the speaker's emotions and feelings, often with songlike qualities.

Lyric poetry began as a fixture of ancient Greece and was a popular form of poetry during the Greco-Roman era, as were dramas (written in verse) and epic poems. The lyric was far shorter, distinguished also by its focus on the poet's state of mind and personal themes rather than a narrative arc. Designed to be sung, lyric poems were typically accompanied by the lyre, a harp-like instrument from which lyric poetry derives its name. Today, lyric poetry encompasses a variety of forms in non-narrative poetry, including the sonnet, elegy, and ode. See also ode and sonnet.

**Metaphor** a comparison between essentially unlike things or the application of a name or description to something to which it is not literally applicable.

Metaphor comes from the Greek word *metaphora* meaning "a transfer" in the sense of carrying over, altering, or changing the essence of one word to a different word. Metaphor is distinct from simile, another element of figurative language that compares two unlike things, in that metaphor does not use the words "like" or "as" in its comparison. Metaphor uses imagery to create a vivid picture by comparing two seemingly different things to each other, thus establishing a connection between the two.

**Meter** the measured pattern of rhythmic accents in a line of verse.

Meter, also known as metre, means the arrangement of language in measured rhythmic movements. The word comes from the Greek word *metron*, which means "measure." Meter is composed of a particular number of syllables found in a single line of poetry, and can be grouped into sets of two or three beats, also known as feet. Feet are units of stressed (also known as accented) and unstressed (unaccented).

## Types of Feet in Poetry

### Two Syllables

Iamb: a metrical foot containing two syllables, the first of which is unstressed and the second of which is stressed (e.g., today).

Trochee: a metrical foot containing two syllables, the first of which is stressed and the second of which is unstressed (e.g., matter).

Spondee: a less common metrical foot in which two consecutive syllables are stressed (e.g., Al).

### Three Syllables

Anapest: a metrical foot containing three syllables, the first two of which are unstressed and the last of which is stressed (e.g., unaware).

Dactyl: a metrical foot containing three syllables, the first stressed and the following two unstressed (e.g., Waverly).

Each line of poetry has a number of feet, and meter refers to that number of feet used in a poetic line. Meter can vary or be consistent throughout a poem. Rising meter contains metrical feet that move from unstressed to stressed syllables, whereas falling meter contains metrical feet that move from stressed to unstressed syllables.

## Types of Meters in Poetry

The length of poetic meter is described using Greek prefixes and suffixes:

Monometer—one foot, one beat per line

Dimeter—two feet, two beats per line

Trimeter—three feet, three beats per line

Tetrameter—four feet, four beats per line

Pentameter—five feet, five beats per line

Hexameter—six feet, six beats per line

Heptameter—seven feet, seven beats per line

Octameter—eight feet, eight beats per line

**Nature poetry** poetry that engages with, describes, or considers the natural world.

Nature poetry is a poetic genre popularized by the Romantic poets, including William Blake, John Keats, and William Wordsworth. Nature poetry expresses ideas, emotions, and situations that have to do with the natural world. There can also be a spiritual quality to nature poetry, as seen in the work of transcendentalist writers Ralph Waldo Emerson and Henry David Thoreau. Nature poems can be written in free verse, or they can contain a specific meter and rhyme scheme. Environmental poetry is a modern extension of nature poetry, where contemporary poets writing about nature focus on environmental issues that address the adverse effects human actions have on the natural environment.

**Nocturne** a poem set at night.

Nocturne is from the French *nocturne*, meaning "composition appropriate to the evening or night." Similar to the musical composition, the nocturne is a poetic form that evokes feelings common to the night such as melancholy, reverie, prayer, sleeplessness, and solitude. Nocturnes are distinct from aubades, which are early morning songs that traditionally describe the parting of lovers. Nocturnes originated in the seventeenth century and continue to be used by contemporary poets to write about the night.

**Ode** a lyric address to an event, a person, or a thing not present.

Ode comes from the Greek *aeidein*, meaning to sing or chant, and belongs to the long and varied tradition of lyric poetry. Traditionally, odes were accompanied by music and dance; later odes became a favored poetic form of Romantic poets such as John Keats and William Wordsworth. There are three general types of odes: the Pindaric, Horatian, and Irregular. The Pindaric is named for the ancient Greek poet Pindar, and contains a strict metrical structure throughout its three sections. The Horatian ode, named for the Roman poet Horace, also has a set metrical structure, whereas the Irregular ode contains no set metrical or rhyme system.

**Pastoral** a creative tradition, as well as individual work idealizing rural life and landscapes.

Viewed alternately as a genre, mode, or convention in literature, art, and music, the pastoral tradition can be traced to Hesiod, a Greek oral poet active between 750 and 650 BC, roughly the same time as Homer. The first written examples of pastoral literature are commonly attributed to the Greek poet Theocritus, who in the third century BC wrote idylls, or short poems describing bucolic life. The conventions of the pastoral genre have evolved from idealized imagery about rural life to imagery that functions as a critique of industrialization and city life.

**Persona poem** a poem in which the poet assumes the voice of another person, fictional character, or identity.

Also known as a dramatic monologue, this form shares many characteristics of a theatrical monologue: An audience is implied; there is no dialogue, and the poet takes on the voice of a character, fictional identity, or persona. Because a dramatic monologue is by definition one person's speech, it is offered without overt analysis or commentary, placing emphasis on subjective qualities and leaving the reader to understand the speaker as they reveal their character and behavior throughout the poem. The dramatic monologue achieved its first era of distinction with the work of Victorian poet Robert Browning, whose deft mastery of the form remains unparalleled.

**Personification** the attribution of human qualities to animals, inanimate objects, or abstract ideas.

Personification has been used in poetry since ancient times, with Homer's *Iliad* and *Odyssey* as examples. Personification is often used in symbolic poetry or allegory, where human characteristics endowed to animals or inanimate objects tell a story, teach a lesson, or represent a different or deeper meaning. Personification was frequently used in the morality plays popular in the fifteenth and sixteenth centuries.

**Poetic diction** the language, including word choice and syntax, that sets poetry apart from other forms of writing.

Poetic diction describes the dialectic and linguistic styles used to write poetry. According to Romantic poet William Wordsworth, poetic diction is the common language of the people in that it must be instinctive and spontaneous. In some languages, poetic diction pertains more to the dialectal use and selection of words for poetic composition. Traditionally, in English poetry, poetic diction mirrored elements of classical poetry, including the use of metaphors and the floral language that often accompanied descriptive imagery. Although Wordsworth strove to redefine poetic diction, modernist poets like Ezra Pound rejected poetic diction and renounced the use of superfluous language such as adjectives to ensure that a poem remained syntactically concise.

**Point of view** the perspective or viewpoint of the speaker in a poem.

*First-person point of view:* The speaker is the one narrating events, providing descriptions, and revealing the poem's content. In storytelling or narrative poetry, the main character is the narrator. The singular first-person point of view relies on the usage of "I" and the plural first-person point of view relies on the usage of "we." Using the first-person point of view in poetry allows the author to create instant intimacy and to evoke a desired emotional bond between the speaker and reader.

*Second-person point of view:* The speaker of a poem tells a story about "you," or describes a series of events, actions, and scenes that include "you." Imperative verbs, actions the speaker wants someone else to do, permeate throughout the poem and influence the poem's tone. The second-person point of view immerses the reader in the poem's content and is implicated in a way that holds the intimate bond between the speaker and the reader.

*Third-person point of view:* The speaker of the poem is not actively part of the story, but is in control of delivering the details. The third-person limited voice can neither describe the internal landscape of any character nor be "in the know" about what the characters are thinking. Third-person omniscient is when the speaker "knows" and describes the internal world of characters while not being part of the story.

**Political poetry** poetry that is related to activism, protest, and social concern, or that is commenting on social, political, or current events.

Political poetry is poetry of social concern and conscience, politically engaged poetry. The feeling often runs high in the social poetry of engagement, especially when it is partisan. Poets write on both sides of any given war, defend the state, attack it. All patriotic and nationalistic poetry is by definition political. Political poetry, ancient and modern, good and bad, frequently responds vehemently to social injustice. There is an ephemeral quality to a lot of political poetry, but a political poem need not be a didactic poem. It can be a poem of testimony and memory.

**Praise poem** a poem of tribute or gratitude.

Praise poetry is part of the literary tradition of many African and European cultures. For example, praise poems in Yorùbá are called *oriki*, in Zulu *isibongo*, and in Tswana *maboko*. In African literary tradition, a praise poem also refers to a series of laudatory epithets applied to gods, people, animals, places, etc., that captures the essence of being praised. These poems are an important part of an oral tradition; professional bards—who may be both praise singers to a chief and court historians of their tribe—chant the poems. These poems offer imagery and storytelling related to a person or subject, and were popular in medieval and Renaissance literature where praise poems expressed worship of or admiration for heroes, kings, or deities.

**Prose poem** a poem that lacks the line breaks traditionally associated with poetry.

Though the name of the form may appear to be a contradiction, the prose poem essentially appears as prose but reads like poetry. While it lacks the line breaks associated with poetry, the prose poem maintains a poetic quality, often utilizing techniques common to poetry, such as fragmentation, compression, repetition, and rhyme. The prose poem can range in length from a few lines to several pages long, and it may explore a limitless array of styles and subjects.

**Quatrain** a four-line stanza, or unit of four lines of verse, rhymed or unrhymed.

Quatrain is diminutive of *quatre*, the French word for four. A quatrain, or four-line stanza, is commonly used in poetry, particularly in sonnets. Quatrains can be unrhymed or appear in rhyme schemes such as ABAB, where the first and third lines and the second and fourth lines rhyme. Other rhyme schemes for quatrains include AABA, AABB, ABBA, ABAC, and ABCB.

## Four Examples of Quatrains in Poetry

Ballad—ABAB, written in iambic pentameter

Double couplet—AABB

Envelope—ABBA

Heroic, also known as Elegiac—ABAB, written in iambic pentameter

See also line, meter, and stanza.

**Revision** both a noun and a verb, revision can refer to the act of making a new, amended, improved, or up-to-date version of a text, or to that version itself.

From the Latin *revidere*, "to look at again," which contains the prefix *re-*, meaning "again" and root word *videre*, "to see," revision is the act of rearranging a text. Revision frequently refers to an author's, poet's, or artist's process of developing their own work, but can also refer to the tradition of reinterpreting or updating an older, perhaps outdated, text.

**Repetition** the poetic technique of repeating the same word or phrase multiple times within a poem.

Repetition is a literary device that predates writings from the tenth century BC. The recurrence of words or phrases throughout a poem influences the poem's tone, mood, rhythm, syntax, and structure. Repetition is found in free verse, but certain poetic forms such as the sestina or villanelle require the fundamental literary device.

## Seven Examples of Repetition in Poetry

Anadiplosis—When a word or phrase is used at the end of one line or clause, and begins the other.

Anaphora—When a word or phrase is repeated at the beginning of each line or clause.

Antistrophe—When a word or phrase is repeated at the end of each line or clause.

Chiasmus—When a word or phrase is repeated in reverse order within a line or clause.

Epimone—When a word or phrase is repeated for the purpose of dwelling on an emotion; this device is usually used in dialogue.

Epizeuxis, also known as diacope—When words or phrases are repeated next to each other or in quick succession within a line or clause.

Symploce—When anaphora and antistrophe are used simultaneously so that a word or phrase is repeated at the beginning of each line or clause and that word or phrase is repeated at the end of each line or clause.

**Rhyme** the correspondence of sounds in words or lines of verse.

Rhyme is often considered a defining feature of poetry, but it is a relatively new technique. The earliest surviving evidence of rhyming dates back to China in the tenth century BC. Rhymes are characterized by the syllables of the words and the placement of the words in a line or stanza. Perfect rhyme occurs if the words' final stressed vowel and all following sounds are identical. For example, bright and flight are perfect rhymes. Poetry usually uses end rhyme, the rhyming of the final syllables of a pair or group of lines. When two words in the same line rhyme, it's called internal rhyme. Poets might also use slant rhyme, which describes words that sound similar but don't exactly rhyme, such as young and long.

**Simile** a comparison between two essentially unlike things using words "such as," "like," and "as."

Simile, similar to metaphor, is another type of figurative language that is used in poetry to establish imagery by creating a vivid picture of how an object, person, or action might appear. Comparing one object to another seemingly unlike object establishes a connection between the two. Simile relies on the use of "like" or "as" to establish equivalency between two things, even if the things aren't literally the same.

**Sonnet** a fourteen-line poem, traditionally written in iambic pentameter, that employs one of several rhyme schemes and adheres to a tightly structured thematic organization.

The sonnet is a popular classical form taken from the Italian *sonetto*, which means "a little sound or song." Two sonnet forms provide the model from which all other sonnets derive: the Petrarchan and the Shakespearean. The Petrarchan sonnet, named after the Italian poet Petrarch, is divided into two stanzas: an octave (the first eight lines) and an answering sestet (the final six lines). The rhyme scheme of the octave is typically ABBAABBA, while the sestet's rhyme scheme is typically CDECDE or CDCDCD, although other sestet variations exist. The Shakespearean sonnet, or English sonnet, consists of three quatrains and a couplet with the rhyme scheme: ABAB, CDCD, EFEF, GG. Within the sonnet form, the volta plays a pivotal role, providing the turn and transition of the poem's tone and central themes.

**Speaker** the voice of a poem, similar to a narrator in fiction.

The speaker can be considered the storyteller or narrator of a poem. The narrative, emotions, and images in a poem are conveyed through the speaker. The poet might not necessarily be the speaker of the poem. Sometimes the poet will write from a different perspective or use the voice of a specific person, as in a persona poem. The term "speaker" clarifies the distinction between the poet's perspective and the perspective used in the poem. In some poems, the distinction between poet and speaker may not be obvious if there are no specific context clues to indicate that the voice narrating the poem has different characteristics from the person writing the poem.

**Spoken word** a broad category of poetry focused on the aesthetics of sound, performance, and recitation.

Spoken word poetry is a twentieth-century art form arising out of the poetic oral tradition, and can be used to refer to any poetic form with an emphasis on euphony, wordplay, and the art of recitation. With roots in the Harlem Renaissance, the civil rights movement, and the Nuyorican Poets Cafe in 1970s New York, spoken word poetry often deals with issues of race, social justice, and community. Spoken word poets may draw on elements of other performance traditions, including hip-hop, jazz, blues, folk music, theater, improvisation, storytelling, dance, and more to communicate to and connect with the audience.

**Stanza** a group of lines that form the basic unit of a poem.

In Italian, the word *stanza* means "room" or "standing, stopping place." Each stanza in a poem is a distinct unit like a room in a house. The number of lines in a stanza can vary, and each stanza within a poem typically has a specific tone and features. In free verse and contemporary poetry, a stanza resembles a prose paragraph in that it can also be used to mark a shift in mood, thought, and place. Stanzas are written according to Latin numerical values.

## Types of Stanzas in Poetry

Monostich: One-line stanza

Couplet: Two-line stanza

Tercet: Three-line stanza

Quatrain: Four-line stanza

Quintet (also known as a quintain): Five-line stanza

Sestet: Six-line stanza

Septet: Seven-line stanza

Octave (also known as an octet): Eight-line stanza

**Syllabic verse** a poetic form that has a fixed or constrained number of syllables per line as well as per stanza.

The meter of syllabic verse poetry is determined by the number of syllables per line, rather than the number of stresses. Syllabic verse disregards the foot–meter system and is found in common poetic forms such as the haiku and tanka. Traditionally, syllabic verse was used in syllable-timed languages, such as French, Japanese, and Spanish, but not in stress-timed languages such as English and German. In the twentieth century, British poets Robert Bridges, Elizabeth Daryush, and Dylan Thomas—among others—pioneered this poetic form. American poets who adopted syllabic verse as their standard metric system include James Laughlin and Marianne Moore.

**Symbol** an object or action that stands for something beyond itself.

Symbol comes from the Greek *symbolon*, an identity token which was verified by comparing it to its other half, from which it gained its contemporary meaning, "something that stands for or suggests something else." Like a metaphor, a symbol compares two ideas or things, but unlike in which two ideas or things are directly connected within the poem or text, a symbol relies on the reader's knowledge or attention to make the extra- or intratextual connection.

**Syntax** the arrangement of language and order of words used to convey the poem's content.

Syntax stems directly from the Greek *syntassein*, which contains the preface *syn-* meaning "together" and *tassein* "arrange." Syntax also comes from the French *syntaxe*, which means the "systematic arrangement of parts," and specifically to grammar, "construction of sentences, arrangement of words." Syntax differs from diction because the device encompasses the unique placement of words together and grammatical conventions employed by the poet, not the word choice in a given sentence or word order. Syntax also produces the poem's rhythm through the repetition of words and sounds, and through the creation of meter.

**Tone** a literary device that conveys the author's attitude toward the subject, speaker, or audience of a poem.

All forms of writing have a tone. Tone is sometimes referred to as the mood of a poem, and can be established through figurative language and imagery. Tone in poetry can range from formal to informal, aggressive to defensive, sentimental to critical, and more. Tone allows the reader to better understand, and even relate to, the speaker's attitude toward the subject of a poem.

**Translation** the art of transferring meaning from one language to another.

Translation comes from the Latin *translatio*, which means "a transferring" or "a carrying over." Translation converts the meaning found in one language (the source language) to another language (the target language), paying close attention to the grammatical rules, vocabulary, and sentence structures of the text. Translation is a communication technology that can be a literal translation, or a freer one that brings the original text to life in the target language without losing any of the meaning and message found in the source language.

**Voice** an expression denoting the comprehensive style of a speaker adopted by the author in a poem.

Voice is what distinguishes poets from each other. A poet may define and construct their literary voice through their unique combination of syntax, poetic diction, repetition, sound, rhyme, form, meter, rhythm, imagery and tone.

# Poet Biographies

**Elizabeth Alexander** was born in Harlem, New York, in 1962 and grew up in Washington, D.C. She is a poet, memoirist, and cultural critic. Alexander's collections of poetry include *Crave Radiance: New and Selected Poems 1990–2010* (Graywolf Press, 2010) and *American Sublime* (Graywolf Press, 2005), which was a finalist for the Pulitzer Prize. Her many honors include the 2007 Jackson Poetry Prize from *Poets & Writers*, as well as fellowships from the Guggenheim Foundation and the National Endowment for the Arts. She served as Chancellor of the Academy of American Poets from 2014 to 2019. She is the current president of the Andrew W. Mellon Foundation and lives in New York City.

**Richard Blanco** was born on February 15, 1968, in Madrid. He is a poet, memoirist, and the Education Ambassador of the Academy of American Poets. He is the author of *Homeland of My Body: New and Selected Poems* (Beacon Press, 2023), among other works. Blanco has taught at various universities and is an associate professor of English at Florida International University. In 2013, Blanco was selected to read at Barack Obama's second presidential inauguration. He was appointed poet laureate of Miami-Dade County in 2022 and was honored with the 2021 National Humanities Medal in 2023. He lives in Bethel, Maine.

**Elizabeth Bradfield** grew up in Tacoma, Washington. Bradfield is the author of five poetry collections, most recently *Toward Antarctica* (Boreal Books, 2019) and *Interpretive Work* (Arktoi Books, 2008), and winner of the Audre Lorde Prize for Lesbian Poetry. She has received fellowships and scholarships from Stanford University's Wallace Stegner Fellowship program, the Bread Loaf Writers' Conference, and Vermont Studio Center. A resident of Cape Cod, Massachusetts, Bradfield works as a naturalist. She teaches creative writing at Brandeis University.

**Jericho Brown** grew up in Shreveport, Louisiana. He is author of multiple books of poetry, including *The Tradition* (Copper Canyon, 2019), which won the Pulitzer Prize, and *Please* (New Issues, 2008), which won the American Book Award. He is the recipient of fellowships from the Guggenheim Foundation, the Radcliffe Institute for Advanced Study at Harvard, and the National Endowment for the Arts. His honors include a Whiting Award and the Academy of American Poets Fellowship in 2022. He was elected Chancellor of the Academy of American Poets in 2024. He is a professor at Emory University and the director of its creative writing program.

**Mahogany L. Browne** was born in Oakland, California. She is a writer, playwright, organizer, and educator. She is the author of several poetry collections and chapbooks, including *Chrome Valley* (W. W. Norton, 2023), winner of the 2024 Paterson Poetry Prize. Browne is the executive director of Bowery Poetry Club, artistic director of Urban Word NYC, and poetry coordinator at St. Francis College. She is also the founder of Woke Baby Book Fair and lives in Brooklyn.

**Carlos Bulosan** was born in the Philippines in 1913. A novelist, poet, and activist, Bulosan emigrated to the United States when he was seventeen. He is best known for *America Is in the Heart* (Harcourt, Brace and Co. Inc., 1946) his semi-autobiographical novel, though he also authored multiple plays, short stories, poems, and novels, including *The Cry and the Dedication* (Temple University Press, 1995), which was published posthumously, and *The Laughter of My Father* (Harcourt, Brace, 1944). Through his work as an anti-colonial activist and labor organizer, Bulosan became a central figure in Filipino American history. He died on September 11, 1956, in Seattle, Washington.

**Lucille Clifton** was born on June 27, 1936, in Depew, New York. She was the author of several poetry collections, including *Blessing the Boats: New and Selected Poems 1988–2000* (BOA Editions, 2000), which won the National Book Award, and *Good Woman: Poems and a Memoir 1969–1980* (BOA Editions, 1987), which was nominated for the Pulitzer Prize. Her other honors include a Lannan Literary Award, two fellowships from the National Endowment for the Arts, and the 2007 Ruth Lilly Poetry Prize. She served as the poet laureate of Maryland from 1979 to 1985, and she was a Chancellor of the Academy of American Poets from 1999 to 2004. Clifton died in Baltimore on February 13, 2010.

**Kwame Dawes** was born in Ghana and raised in Kingston, Jamaica. He is a poet, novelist, memoirist, and editor. His works of poetry include *Progeny of Air* (Peepal Tree Press, 1994), which received the Forward Poetry Prize for Best First Collection. His many honors include the Musgrave Silver Medal for contribution to the arts in Jamaica, and the Barnes and Noble Writers for Writers Award from Poets & Writers. He served as a Chancellor of the Academy of American Poets from 2018 to 2023. He is founding director of the African Poetry Book Fund and the poet laureate of Jamaica from 2024 to 2027.

**Tyree Daye** was raised in Youngsville, North Carolina. He is the author of the poetry collections *a little bump in the earth* (Copper Canyon Press, 2024), *Cardinal* (Copper Canyon Press, 2020), and *River Hymns* (American Poetry Review, 2017), and winner of the APR/Honickman First Book Prize. Daye is also the recipient of a Whiting Award and is an assistant professor at the University of North Carolina at Chapel Hill.

**Natalie Diaz** was born in 1978 and raised in the Fort Mojave Indian Village in Needles, California. Both Mojave and an enrolled member of the Gila River Indian Tribe, she is the author of *Postcolonial Love Poem* (Graywolf Press, 2020), winner of the Pulitzer Prize, and *When My Brother Was an Aztec* (Copper Canyon Press, 2012), winner of an American Book Award. Diaz has received fellowships from the MacArthur Foundation, the Lannan Literary Foundation, and the Native Arts Council Foundation. She was elected a Chancellor of the Academy of American Poets in 2021. She lives in Phoenix, Arizona.

**Rita Dove** was born in Akron, Ohio, in 1952. She is a poet, novelist, and editor. Her books of poetry include *Collected Poems 1974–2004* (W. W. Norton, 2016), recipient of the 2017 NAACP Image Award; *Sonata Mulattica* (W. W. Norton, 2009), winner of the Hurston/Wright Legacy Award; and *Thomas and Beulah* (Carnegie Mellon University Press, 1986), which won the 1987 Pulitzer Prize. She received the Wallace Stevens Award from the Academy of American Poets in 2019. Dove served as poet laureate of the United States from 1993 to 1995, poet laureate of Virginia from 2004 to 2006, and Chancellor of the Academy of American Poets from 2005 to 2010. She currently serves as the American Academy of Arts and Letters' vice president for literature and is the Henry Hoyns Professor of Creative Writing at the University of Virginia.

**Danielle Legros Georges** was born in Haiti and raised in the United States. She is a poet, editor, and translator. She is the author of four poetry collections, including *Three Leaves, Three Roots: Poems on the Haiti–Congo Story* (Beacon Press, 2025). She also translated the anthology *Blue Flare: Three Haitian Poets: Évelyne Trouillot, Marie-Célie Agnant, Maggy de Coster* (Zephyr Press, 2024). She served as Boston's second poet laureate from 2015 to 2019. She is a professor emeritus in the MFA creative writing program at Lesley University and lives in Boston.

**José B. González** was born in San Salvador, El Salvador, and emigrated to the United States at the age of eight. He received a BS from Bryant University, an MA from Brown University, and a PhD from the University of Rhode Island. González is the author of *When Love Was Reels*

(Arte Público Press, 2017) and *Toys Made of Rock* (Bilingual Press/Editorial Bilingüe, 2015). The recipient of a 2012 Fulbright Scholarship, he is professor of English at the United States Coast Guard Academy and lives in Quaker Hill, Connecticut.

**Kimiko Hahn** was born in 1955 in Mount Kisco, New York. Hahn is the author of ten poetry collections, including *The Ghost Forest: New and Selected Poems* (W. W. Norton, 2024) and *The Unbearable Heart* (Kaya Production, 1995), which received an American Book Award. Her other honors and awards include the Theodore Roethke Memorial Poetry Prize and the 2023 Ruth Lilly Poetry Prize. She is a distinguished professor in the creative writing and literary translation MFA program at Queens College, the City University of New York. Hahn was elected Chancellor of the Academy of American Poets in 2023.

**Joy Harjo** is a member of the Muscogee/Creek Nation and was born in Tulsa, Oklahoma, in 1951. She is a poet, musician, and playwright. In 1978, she received an MFA from the Iowa Writers' Workshop. In 2019, Harjo became the first Native American to be appointed U.S. poet laureate. She served as Chancellor of the Academy of American Poets from 2019 to 2024. Harjo is the author of numerous books of poetry, including *Weaving Sundown in a Scarlet Light: 50 Poems for 50 Years* (W. W. Norton, 2022). She was awarded the 2015 Wallace Stevens Award from the Academy of American Poets and the 2023 Bollingen Prize for Poetry in recognition of lifetime achievement in and contributions to American poetry. She lives on the Muscogee Nation Reservation in Oklahoma.

**Joy Ladin** was born in 1961. She is a poet and memoirist. Ladin has published numerous poetry collections, including the revised second edition of *The Book of Anna* (EOAGH, 2021), which won the National Jewish Book Award. Ladin is also the author of a memoir, *Through the Door of Life: A Jewish Journey Between Genders* (University of Wisconsin Press, 2012). She is the recipient of a National Endowment for the Arts Fellowship, a Hadassah-Brandeis Research Award, and a Fulbright Scholarship. In 2007, she became the first openly transgender employee of Yeshiva University, an Orthodox Jewish institution.

**Joseph O. Legaspi** was born in the Philippines, where he lived before immigrating to Los Angeles with his family at age twelve. He received an MFA from New York University's Creative Writing Program. Legaspi is the author of *Imago* (CavanKerry Press, 2007), winner of a Global Filipino Literary Award. In 2004, he cofounded Kundiman, a national organization serving Asian American writers and readers. He lives in Queens, New York.

**Ali Liebegott** is a poet, novelist, and screenwriter. She is the author of the novel-in-verse *The Summer of Dead Birds, 2013* (Amethyst Editions, 2019), and the novels *Cha-Ching!* (City Lights, 2013) and *The*

*IHOP Papers* (Carroll & Graf, 2007). Her honors include two Lambda Literary Awards in Women's Fiction and Lesbian Debut Fiction, as well as a poetry fellowship from the New York Foundation of the Arts. She received a Peabody Award for her work as a writer for the show *Transparent*. She lives in Los Angeles, California.

**Queen Lili'uokalani** was born on September 2, 1838, in Honolulu, Hawai'i, as Lydia Lili'u Loloku Walania Wewehi Kamaka'eha. She was proclaimed queen in 1891. The last monarch of Hawai'i, her reign was short-lived due to a U.S. military-backed coup in 1893. After an unsuccessful attempt to restore Queen Lili'uokalani to power, she was sentenced to five years in prison at hard labor, which later became imprisonment in a bedroom of Iolani Palace for eight months. A gifted songwriter, she wrote and composed more than 160 songs, including "Aloha Oe" (Farewell to Thee). Lili'uokalani continued to fight for a free Hawai'i until her death on November 11, 1917.

**Ada Limón** was born in 1976 in Sonoma, California. She is the author of six books of poetry, including *The Carrying* (Milkweed Editions, 2018), which won the National Book Critics Circle Award, and *The Hurting Kind* (Milkweed Editions, 2022), which was short-listed for the Griffin Poetry Prize. She is the twenty-fourth poet laureate of the United States. Limón is also the recipient of a MacArthur Fellowship and was named a *Time* magazine woman of the year.

**Yesenia Montilla**, born and raised in New York City, is an Afro-Latina poet and a daughter of immigrants. She received her MFA from Drew University in poetry and poetry in translation. She is the author of *Muse Found in a Colonized Body* (Four Way Books, 2022), which was nominated for an NAACP Image Award, and *The Pink Box* (Aquarius Press, 2015), which was long-listed for the PEN Open Book Award. The recipient of fellowships from CantoMundo and the New York Foundation for the Arts, Montilla lives in Harlem, New York.

**Kamilah Aisha Moon** was born in Nashville, Tennessee in 1973. Moon authored the poetry collections *Starshine & Clay* (Four Way Books, 2017) and *She Has a Name* (Four Way Books, 2013), which was a finalist for the Lambda Literary Award for Lesbian Poetry and the Audre Lorde Award from The Publishing Triangle. Moon's other honors included fellowships from Cave Canem, Fine Arts Work Center, MacDowell, and Vermont Studio Center. She taught at Agnes Scott College in Atlanta, where she lived until her passing on September 24, 2021.

**Marilyn Nelson** was born in Cleveland, Ohio, in 1946. Nelson's books include *The Fields of Praise: New and Selected Poems* (Louisiana State University Press, 1997), which was a finalist for the 1997 National Book Award, and *The Homeplace* (Louisiana State University Press, 1990), which won the 1992 Anisfield-Wolf Award. Nelson's honors include a Frost Medal from the Poetry Society of America, the 2019 Ruth Lilly Poetry Prize, the 2019 Denise Levertov Award, and the 2022 Wallace

Stevens Award from the Academy of American Poets. She served as the poet laureate of Connecticut from 2001 to 2006 and as Chancellor of the Academy of American Poets from 2012 to 2017.

**Naomi Shihab Nye** was born in St. Louis, Missouri, in 1952. She is the author of numerous collections of poetry, including *You and Yours* (BOA Editions, 2005), which received the Isabella Gardner Poetry Award. She is also the author of several children's books, including *Habibi* (Simon Pulse, 1997), which won the Jane Addams Children's Book Award. Nye served as Chancellor of the Academy of American Poets from 2009 to 2014 and received the 2019 Ivan Sandrof Lifetime Achievement Award from the National Book Critics Circle and the Wallace Stevens Award from the Academy of American Poets in 2024. She lives in San Antonio, Texas.

**Wang Ping** was born in Shanghai in 1957 during the Cultural Revolution and immigrated to the United States in 1985. She is an author and poet. Ping's poetry collections include *Ten Thousand Waves* (Wings Press, 2014), *The Magic Whip* (Coffee House Press, 2003), and *Of Flesh & Spirit* (Coffee House Press, 1998). Ping's awards include fellowships from the Bush Foundation, the New York Foundation for the Arts, and the National Endowment for the Arts. She is a professor emerita at Macalester College in St. Paul, Minnesota.

**Alexander Posey**, born August 3, 1873, was a Muscogee Creek poet, journalist, and humorist known for his poems and Fus Fixico letters, a series of satirical letters written from his fictional persona, Fus Fixico, that commented on the local and national politics of his time. He served as the editor for the *Eufaula Indian Journal* before passing away on May 27, 1908. *The Poems of Alexander Lawrence Posey* (Crane Printers), collected and arranged by Posey's wife, was published posthumously in 1910.

**Minnie Bruce Pratt** was born in 1946 in Selma, Alabama, and grew up in Centreville, Alabama. Her books of poetry include *The Dirt She Ate: Selected and New Poems* (University of Pittsburgh Press, 2003), winner of the Lambda Literary Award in Lesbian Poetry, and *Crime Against Nature* (Firebrand Books, 1990), which received the Academy of American Poets' Lamont Poetry Selection and the American Library Association's Gay and Lesbian Book Award for Literature. She died on July 2, 2023.

**Roger Reeves** earned his PhD from the University of Texas at Austin and is the author of *Dark Days: Fugitive Essays* (Graywolf Press, 2023); *Best Barbarian* (W. W. Norton, 2022), winner of the 2023 Kingsley Tufts Poetry Award; and *King Me* (Copper Canyon Press, 2013), winner of the Larry Levis Reading Prize. Reeves is also the recipient of the 2023 Griffin Poetry Prize and a Whiting Award, as well as fellowships from Cave Canem, the National Endowment for the Arts, the Poetry Foundation, and Princeton University.

# Poet Biographies

**Alberto Alvaro Ríos** was born on September 18, 1952, in Nogales, Arizona. He is a poet, memoirist, and novelist. His poetry collections include *The Theater of Night* (Copper Canyon Press, 2005), winner of the 2007 PEN/Beyond Margins Award, and *The Smallest Muscle in the Human Body* (Copper Canyon Press, 2002), a finalist for the National Book Award. Ríos served as Chancellor of the Academy of American Poets from 2013 to 2018. He is the Piper Center Director and Professor at Arizona State University and serves as Arizona's inaugural poet laureate.

**Mary Jo Salter** was born in 1954 in Grand Rapids, Michigan, and grew up in Baltimore, Maryland. A poet, children's book author, and lyricist, her poetry collections include *Nothing by Design* (Alfred A. Knopf, 2013), *A Phone Call to the Future* (Alfred A. Knopf, 2008), and *Open Shutters* (Alfred A. Knopf, 2003). She has received honors from the Guggenheim Foundation, the National Endowment for the Arts, and the Rockefeller Foundation, among others. A member of the American Academy of Arts and Sciences, she was the vice president of the Poetry Society of America from 1995 to 2007. She lives in Baltimore.

**Tracy K. Smith** was born in 1972 in Falmouth, Massachusetts, and raised in California. She is a poet, memoirist, editor, translator, and librettist. Her books of poetry include *Wade in the Water* (Graywolf Press, 2018), winner of the 2019 Anisfield-Wolf Book Award in Poetry, and *Life on Mars* (Graywolf Press, 2011), winner of the 2012 Pulitzer Prize. She served as the twenty-second poet laureate of the United States from 2017 to 2019. In 2021, she was elected as Chancellor of the Academy of American Poets.

**Ocean Vuong** was born in Ho Chi Minh City, Vietnam, in 1988, immigrated to the United States at the age of two, and was raised in Hartford, Connecticut. He is a poet and novelist. His poetry collections are *Time Is a Mother* (Penguin Press, 2022) and *Night Sky with Exit Wounds* (Copper Canyon Press, 2016), which received the 2017 Felix Dennis Prize for Best First Collection from the Forward Arts Foundation and the T. S. Eliot Prize. Vuong has received numerous other honors, including a Ruth Lilly and Dorothy Sargent Rosenberg Poetry Fellowship and a Whiting Award. In 2019, he was named a recipient of the MacArthur Fellowship. He teaches in the Creative Writing Program at New York University.

# Credits

Elizabeth Alexander, "Haircut" from *Crave Radiance: New and Selected Poems 1990–2010* (Graywolf Press, 1997) by Elizabeth Alexander. Copyright © 1997 by Elizabeth Alexander. Used with the permission of The Permissions Company LLC on behalf of Graywolf Press, graywolfpress.org.

Richard Blanco, "América" from *City of a Hundred Fires* (University of Pittsburgh Press, 1988), by Richard Blanco. Copyright © 1998 by Richard Blanco. Used with the permission of the University of Pittsburgh Press.

Jericho Brown, "Crossing" from *The Tradition* (Copper Canyon Press, 2019) by Jericho Brown. Copyright © 2019 by Jericho Brown. Used with the permission of The Permissions Company LLC on behalf of Copper Canyon Press, coppercanyonpress.org.

Mahogany L. Browne, "When Fannie Lou Hamer Said" Copyright © 2019 by Mahogany L. Browne. Used with the permission of the author.

Carlos Bulosan, "I Want the Wide American Earth" University of Washington Libraries, Special Collections, Accession 0581-012, Carlos Bulosan Papers, Box 3/17

Lucille Clifton, "won't you celebrate with me" from *The Book of Light* (Copper Canyon Press, 1993) by Lucille Clifton. Copyright © 1993 by Lucille Clifton. Used with the permission of The Permissions Company LLC on behalf of Copper Canyon Press, coppercanyonpress.org.

Kwame Dawes, "Dirt" from *Duppy Conqueror: New and Selected Poems* (Copper Canyon Press, 2013) by Kwame Dawes. Copyright © 2013 by Kwame Dawes. Used with the permission of The Permissions Company LLC on behalf of Copper Canyon Press, coppercanyonpress.org.

Tyree Daye, "Miss Mary Mack Introduces Her Wings" from *Captivity* (Copper Canyon Press, 2020) by Tyree Daye. Copyright © 2020

## Credits

by Tyree Daye. Used with the permission of The Permissions Company LLC on behalf of Copper Canyon Press, coppercanyonpress.org.

Natalie Diaz, "They Don't Love You Like I Love You" from *Postcolonial Love Poem*. (Graywolf Press, 2020) by Natalie Diaz. Copyright © 2020 by Natalie Diaz. Used with the permission of The Permissions Company LLC on behalf of Graywolf Press, graywolfpress.org.

Rita Dove, "Girls on the Town, 1946," from *Playlist for the Apocalypse: Poems* (by W. W. Norton & Company Inc., 2021) by Rita Dove. Copyright © 2021 by Rita Dove. Used with the permission of W. W. Norton & Company Inc.

Kimiko Hahn, "The Dream of Shoji," from *Brain Fever* (W. W. Norton & Company Inc., 2014) by Kimiko Hahn. Copyright © 2014 by Kimiko Hahn. Used with the permission of W. W. Norton & Company Inc.

Joy Harjo, "Perhaps the World Ends Here," from *The Woman Who Fell From The Sky* (W. W. Norton & Company Inc., 1996) by Joy Harjo. Copyright © 1994 by Joy Harjo. Used with the permission of W. W. Norton & Company Inc.

Joy Ladin, "Survival Guide," from *The Future Is Trying to Tell Us Something: New and Selected Poems* (Sheep Meadow Press, 2017). Copyright © 2017 by Joy Ladin. Used with the permission of the publisher.

Joseph O. Legaspi, "Amphibians," Copyright © 2014 Joseph O. Legaspi. Reprinted from *Split This Rock's The Quarry: A Social Justice Poetry Database*. Used with the permission of the poet.

Danielle Legros Georges, "Poem for the Poorest Nation in the Western Hemisphere" Copyright © 2010 Danielle Legros Georges. Used with the permission of the poet.

Ali Liebegott, "Senior Discount," Copyright © 2016 by Ali Liebegott. Originally published in Poem-a-Day on August 30, 2016, by the Academy of American Poets. Used with the permission of the author.

Ada Limón, "A New National Anthem," from *The Carrying* (Milkweed Editions, 2018). Copyright © 2018 by Ada Limón. Used with the permission of The Permissions Company LLC on behalf of Milkweed Editions, milkweed.org.

Yesenia Montilla, "Maps," from *Muse Found in a Colonized Body* (Four Way Books, 2022). Copyright © 2017, 2022 by Yesenia Montilla. Used with permission of The Permissions Company LLC on behalf of Four Way Books, fourwaybooks.com.

Kamilah Aisha Moon, "Imagine," from *Starshine & Clay* (Four Way Books, 2017). Copyright © 2017 by Kamilah Aisha Moon. Used with the permission of The Permissions Company LLC on behalf of Four Way Books, fourwaybooks.com.

Marilyn Nelson, "Making History," Copyright © 2014 Marilyn Nelson. From *Beloit Poetry Journal, Split This Rock Edition*. Reprinted from *Split This Rock's The Quarry: A Social Justice Poetry Database*. Used by permission of the poet.

Wang Ping, "Things We Carry on the Sea," from *My Name Is Immigrant* (Hanging Loose Press, 2020). Copyright © 2020 Wang Ping. Used with the permission of the press.

Minnie Bruce Pratt, "The Cabbage Butterfly," from *Magnified* (Wesleyan University Press, 2021). Copyright © 2021 by Minnie Bruce Pratt. Published by Wesleyan University Press, Middletown, Connecticut. Used with permission.

Alberto Ríos, "A House Called Tomorrow," from *Not Go Away Is My Name* (Copper Canyon Press, 2020). Copyright © 2018, 2020 by Alberto Ríos. Used with the permission of The Permissions Company LLC on behalf of Copper Canyon Press, coppercanyonpress.org.

Mary Jo Salter, "The Buttonhook," from *The Surveyors: Poems* (Alfred A. Knopf, 2017). Copyright © 2017 by Mary Jo Salter. Used by permission of Alfred A. Knopf, an imprint of the Knopf Doubleday Publishing Group, a division of Penguin Random House LLC. All rights reserved.

Tracy K. Smith, "Declaration," from *Such Color: New and Selected Poems* (Graywolf Press, 2018). Originally from *The New Yorker* (November 6, 2017). Copyright © 2017, 2018 by Tracy K. Smith. Used with the permission of The Permissions Company LLC on behalf of Graywolf Press, graywolfpress.org.

Ocean Vuong, "Kissing in Vietnamese," Copyright © 2014 by Ocean Vuong. Originally published in *Split This Rock's The Quarry: A Social Justice Poetry Database*. Reprinted by permission of the author.

# Bibliography

Academy of American Poets. "An interview with Joy Harjo, U.S. Poet Laureate." Poets.org, Academy of American Poets, June 15, 2017. https://poets.org/text/four-questions-us-poet-laureate-tracy-k-smith

African American Pamphlet Collection. The agitation of slavery. Who commenced! And who can end it!! Buchanan and Fillmore compared from the record. [N. P, 1856] Pdf. https://www.loc.gov/item/09004259/

After Action Report. "The battle of hue, 2–26 February 1968." *DocsTeach*, March 10, 1968. https://www.docsteach.org/documents/document/report-battle-hue

Beckwith, Martha Warren. "The Kumulipo: A Hawaiian creation chant." Ulukau: The Hawaiian Electronic Library, n.d. https://puke.ulukau.org/?a=d&d=EBOOK-BECKWIT2.2.1.1&e=-------haw-20--1--txt-txPT-----------

Behizadeh, Nadia, Sarah Bonner, Katie Burnett, Joanne Baird Giordano, Mara Lee Grayson, Jarvais Jackson, and Emily Meixner. "Position statement on supporting teachers and students in discussing complex topics." National Council of Teachers of English, September 12, 2024. https://ncte.org/statement/position-statement-on-supporting-teachers-and-students-in-discussing-complex-topics/

Britannica, T. Editors of Encyclopaedia. "Cherokee language." *Encyclopedia Britannica*, January 10, 2020. https://www.britannica.com/topic/Cherokee-language

Capinera, John L. "Featured creatures: Imported cabbageworm." University of Florida Entomology & Nematology. August 2014. https://entnemdept.ufl.edu/creatures/veg/leaf/imported_cabbageworm.htm#life

Carson, C., and David L. Lewis. "Martin Luther King, Jr." *Encyclopedia Britannica*, October 16, 2024. https://www.britannica.com/biography/Martin-Luther-King-Jr

Chow, Keith. "Building America." The Nerds of Color, May 9, 2014. https://thenerdsofcolor.org/2014/05/09/building-america-by-ming-doyle/

City of Asylum. "The writer's block: A video Q&A with Kwame Dawes." YouTube, February 13, 2017. https://www.youtube.com/watch?v=uX45_sz6LuY

Dewey, John. *Art as Experience*, 18th ed. (New York City: Perigee Books, 1980).

Diaz, Natalie. "A poetry portfolio: Featuring five of our country's finest native poets." Poets.org, Academy of American Poets, November 10, 2015. https://poets.org/text/poetry-portfolio-featuring-five-our-countrys-finest-native-poets

Doty, Mark. "Tide of voices: Why poetry matters now." Poets.org, Academy of American Poets, August 9, 2010. https://poets.org/text/tide-voices-why-poetry-matters-now

Facing History & Ourselves. "Fostering civil discourse: Difficult classroom conversations in a diverse democracy," September 12, 2024. https://www.facinghistory.org/resource-library/fostering-civil-discourse-difficult-classroom-conversations-diverse-democracy

Finefield, Kristi. "Sequoyah: A man of letters." Library of Congress, November 15, 2013. https://blogs.loc.gov/picturethis/2013/11/sequoyah-a-man-of-letters/

Greene, Maxine. *Variations on a Blue Guitar: The Lincoln Center Institute Lectures on Aesthetic Education*. (New York and London: Teachers College Press, 2018).

Hall, Stephaniel. "How Hawaiians saved their language." Library of Congress, May 24, 2017. https://blogs.loc.gov/folklife/2017/05/how-hawaiians-saved-their-language/

Hannah-Jones, Nicole. "The idea of America." The 1619 Project, August 18, 2019. https://pulitzercenter.org/sites/default/files/the_idea_of_america_full_essay.pdf

Harjo, Joy. "Ancestors: A mapping of indigenous poetry and poets." Poets.org, Academy of American Poets, November 24, 2015. https://poets.org/text/ancestors-mapping-indigenous-poetry-and-poets

Hayes, Terrance. "Survey of an American century." Poets.org, Academy of American Poets, September 11, 2020. https://poets.org/text/survey-american-century

Hess, Diana E, and Paula Mcavoy *The Political Classroom: Evidence and Ethics in Democratic Education*. (Routledge, 2015.)

Hirshfield, Jane. *Ten Windows: How Great Poems Transform the World*. (New York City: Alfred A. Knopf, Inc., 2015).

Lamba, Admin. "I am not me: Unmaking and remaking the language of the self." lambdaliterary.org, Lambda Literary, December 28,

# Bibliography

2014. https://lambdaliterary.org/2014/12/unmaking-and-remaking-the-language-of-the-self/

Levin, Dana. "Where it breaks: Drama, silence, speed, and accrual." Poets.org, Academy of American Poets, February 20, 2014. https://poets.org/text/where-it-breaks-drama-silence-speed-and-accrual

National Park Service. "Emma Lazarus." NPS.gov, National Park Service, March 29, 2024. https://www.nps.gov/people/emma-lazarus.htm

NPR. "Renisha McBride Shooting: 'We may never know' why." November 18, 2013. https://www.npr.org/2013/11/18/245967473/renisha-mcbride-shooting-we-may-never-know-why

NPR. "Read Martin Luther King Jr.'s 'I have a dream' speech in its entirety." January 16, 2023. https://www.npr.org/2010/01/18/122701268/i-have-a-dream-speech-in-its-entirety

Nye, Naomi Shihab. "Video: Naomi Shihab Nye on the poet's civic responsibility." Poets.org, Academy of American Poets, September 29, 2015. https://poets.org/text/video-naomi-shihab-nye-poets-civic-responsibility

PFLAG. "LGBTQ+ glossary." PFLAG. 2023. https://pflag.org/glossary/

Reiss, Aaron, Emily Rhyne, and Todd Heisler. "Around the world in 5 kids' game." *The New York Times*, December 6, 2019. https://www.nytimes.com/interactive/2019/12/06/arts/kids-games.html

Ríos, Alberto. "Some thoughts on the integrity of the single line in poetry." Poets.org. Academy of American Poets, February 20, 2011. https://poets.org/text/some-thoughts-integrity-single-line-poetry

Ruffin II, Herbert G. "Black lives matter: The growth of a new social justice movement." Blackpast.org, BlackPast, August 23, 2015. https://www.blackpast.org/african-american-history/black-lives-matter-growth-new-social-justice-movement/

Sanchez, Sanchez, and Major Jackson. "Video: Sonia Sanchez and Major Jackson on legacy and the joys of teaching." Poets.org, Academy of American Poets, August 31, 2017. https://poets.org/text/video-sonia-sanchez-and-major-jackson-legacy-and-joys-teaching

Segal, Corinne. "How poetry helped Marcelo Hernandez Castillo speak out on immigration." PBS.org, PBS News, March 14, 2016. https://www.pbs.org/newshour/arts/poetry/how-poetry-helped-marcelo-hernandez-castillo-speak-out-on-immigration

Shihab Nye, Naomi. "Video: Naomi Shihab Nye on the poet's civic responsibility." Poets.org, Academy of American Poets, September 29, 2015. https://poets.org/text/video-naomi-shihab-nye-poets-civic-responsibility

# Bibliography

Smith, Roswell Chamberlain. "Page 16." *Smith's Quarto, or Second Book in Geography. A Concise and Practical System of Geography.* (University of Michigan Library, 1848a.)

Smith, Roswell Chamberlain. "Page 17." *Smith's Quarto, or Second Book in Geography. A Concise and Practical System of Geography.* (University of Michigan Library, 1848b.)

Stanford University. "Say their names." Spotlight at Stanford, n.d. https://exhibits.stanford.edu/saytheirnames

UNHCR. "Refugee statistics | USA for UNHCR." Unrefugees.org, 2023. https://www.unrefugees.org/refugee-facts/statistics/

University of Washington University Libraries. "Author, poet, and worker: The world of Carlos Bulosan." University of Washington University Libraries. https://content.lib.washington.edu/exhibits/bulosan/index.html

Wick Poetry Center at Kent State University. "Emerge poetry—Here on Earth." February 26, 2021. https://hereonearth.world/emerge-poetry

# Acknowledgments

Teach This Poem would not have existed without the Academy of American Poets, including the Board of Directors, Chancellors, Education Advisory Council, Education Ambassador, and Academy staff past and present, and their dedication and work to fund, support, and produce this important resource year in and out.

The series owes a great deal of gratitude to Jen Benka, former Executive Director and President of the Academy, whose leadership inspired and encouraged me. Mary Gannon, the former Associate Director/Director of Content, made the early concept of Teach This Poem possible, and with Jen, recognized the importance of a print collection of this work. Ansley Moon most ably took over the creation of online lessons in 2019.

Teach This Poem could not have begun without the dedication and feedback from a group of New York City third and fourth grade school teachers, as well as teachers from high schools connected with New Visions for Public Schools. They grounded our ideas, and inspired us with their commitment to teach poetry to their students.

Present Academy Staff Members Kat Rejsek, Nadra Mabrouk, and Jeffery Gleaves lent their talents and diligence to the book's production. Ricardo Alberto Maldonado, the Academy's Executive Director and President, provided continuous support and encouragement.

My greatest thanks to all.

# Author Biography

**Madeleine Fuchs Holzer** was the inaugural Educator in Residence at the Academy of American Poets from 2014 to 2023. She previously served as Educational Development Director and Program Development Director at Lincoln Center Institute for the Arts in Education, where she wrote the Institute's Capacities for Imaginative Learning and other conceptual documents. Prior to that, Holzer was the Director of Arts in Education at the New York State Council on the Arts. Her poetry and essays have been published in *Education Week*, *Black Fly Review*, *Footwork: Paterson Literary Review*, *Pearl*, and *Ibbetson Street* among others. Holzer has taught at Cornell and New York Universities, and at Fox Lane High School in Bedford, New York. In addition, she taught poetry at East Side Community High School in New York City. She was Senior Editor for English/Language Arts at Sunburst Communications, where she developed the award-winning CD-ROMs *Romeo and Juliet: Center Stage* and *In My Own Voice: Multicultural Poets on Identity*. Holzer holds an Ed.D from Teachers College, Columbia University and an MA in English with a concentration in creative writing from New York University. She was a Resident at MacDowell.

For Product Safety Concerns and Information please contact our EU representative GPSR@taylorandfrancis.com
Taylor & Francis Verlag GmbH, Kaufingerstraße 24, 80331 München, Germany

www.ingramcontent.com/pod-product-compliance
Lightning Source LLC
Chambersburg PA
CBHW080925300426
44115CB00018B/2943